Skiing is Believing

The Skier's Psalm

Yea, though I ski through the Valley of the Shadow
of Debt, I shall fear no snowboarder;
Thy lodge and its staff, they comfort me;
Though layest a table before me in the presence of
mine credit card;
Thou anointest my flambé with cognac;
My hottub overflows;
Surely sunshine and short lift lines shall follow me all
the days of my life,
And I shall schuss the slopes on my boards forever.

Skiing is Believing

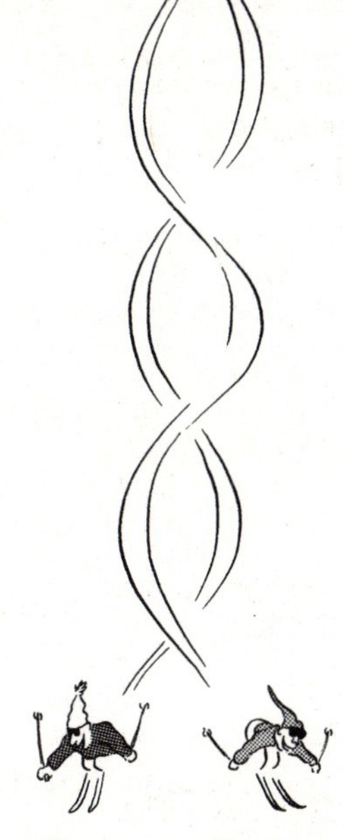

Eric Nicol and Dave More

Johnson Gorman Publishers

The Publishers
Johnson Gorman Publishers
3669 – 41 Avenue
Red Deer Alberta Canada T4N 2X7

Credits
Designed by Full Court Press Inc.
Printed and bound in Canada by Webcom Limited for Johnson Gorman Publishers.

Acknowledgments
Financial support provided by the Alberta Foundation for the Arts, a beneficiary of the Lottery Fund of the Government of Alberta.

COMMITTED TO THE DEVELOPMENT OF CULTURE AND THE ARTS

Canadian Cataloguing in Publication Data
Nicol, Eric, 1919–
Skiing is believing
ISBN 0-921835-23-X
1. Skis and skiing—Humor. I. More, Dave. II. Title.
GV854.3.N52 1996 796.93'0207 C96-910586-X

Contents

To the reader, assuming that he/she bought this copy of the book. –E.N.

To Terry W., who taught me not to be scared of heights. –D.M.

To the Aspirant Skier:

You have your Old Testament, and you have your New Testament, and now you have your *Skiing Is Believing*. Bless you! We, the authors, do not hesitate to call it the bible of skiing. Why? Because this gospel gives the skier a lot more commandments than other bibles that sell for more. There are at least ten no-nos in the first chapter alone. And all the chapters provide to the novice skier what he or she needs most, namely the belief in miracles.

They define the challenge: how to free the spirit from the body, on skis, while still having sex. Without that goal, many neophytes treat skiing as just another sport, rather than a calling from on high (6000 feet). They fail to understand that the ski hill is unforgiving to those who stray from the straight and narrow piste. They fall easy prey to the snowboarder, and occasional very coarse and suggestive language.

To be a good skier, both morally and physically, becomes ever harder as the ski resort comes to be seen as a Club Med with clothes on. Without a robust work ethic—which this book insists on—the learning skier is apt to lapse into that majority of skiers who rarely leave the lounge on flimsy excuse ("I've become allergic to snow") or because they broke their leg.

Don't be discouraged. Once you have learned to ski, you need never do another proper thing. You are a pro. We leave you to Heaven.

—E.N. & D.M.

CHAPTER 1

Genesis of Skiing

Let There Be Light (Powder)

IN THE BEGINNING there was the *skee. Skee* was the English spelling as recently as the nineteenth century, and one is tempted to regret that a relatively clean four-letter word has shrunk to three. A person would expect to have more fun at a skee resort . . . the coupled e's and romance implicit in the après skee . . . .

However. *Ski* is the spelling found in today's *Oxford Concise Dictionary,* which does not encourage license. The word derives from the Old Norse *skith.* (Since philologists disagree on this, the derivation may be a Norse of a different scholar.)

Some say that *ski* comes from the Old Danish, of which vestiges are found in the office cafeteria. *Our* selection is the *very* old Icelandic *skidth,* meaning a snowshoe. This is easy to remember if we think of today's ski slope as the Skidth Row. Especially if we fall down a lot and have to be taken away in a police van.

Did the modern ski evolve from the snowshoe, the way that man is said to have evolved from the ape, so that today the two species coexist but rarely get invited to the same party? Or is the fundamentalist correct in believing that God created skis as His noblest work and would have included them as part of the Garden of Eden, except Adam and Eve were not dressed for alpine events?

This book favors the latter thesis, but feels obliged to note that most anthropologists believe that skis began as the sanded-down bones of a large animal. One has to imagine a couple of Norsemen relaxing on a snow-covered hill after killing and butchering a woolly mammoth . . .

"Vell, Lars, that's it. Ve haf loaded your old pickup sleigh wit everything but the tusks."

"Ja, Sven. My wife says the tusks are too big for soup bones. They leaf no room in the pot for spuds."

"Seems a shame, though, to throw them away."

"Ja. Litter."

"Maybe if ve shave these suckers down a bit wit der sander and tie them to our feet, ve can skidth down the hill and impress chicks."

"Cool, man! Uh, vat's a sander?"

It's a stretch. Until an archeologist discovers a pair of sanded-down animal bones stuck upright in the snow and clearly marked ROSSIGNOL, we remain skeptical.

Another premise: skis were born when an Old Danish beer-barrel maker, having tested beer from several of his barrels, accidentally stepped on a couple of loose staves and took off down a snow-covered slope. This was such fun that he did it again on purpose, rammed into a tree and realized he had found the perfect Christmas gift for his wife and children.

A merry myth. More likely though is that the ski did evolve from the primitive snowshoe. The snowshoe was an early model of a tennis racket that never caught on because nobody had thought of the tennis court, let alone the Adidas court shoes. The snowshoe proved to be a reliable mode of transportation in heavy snow, but a person racing in snowshoes lacked something as a

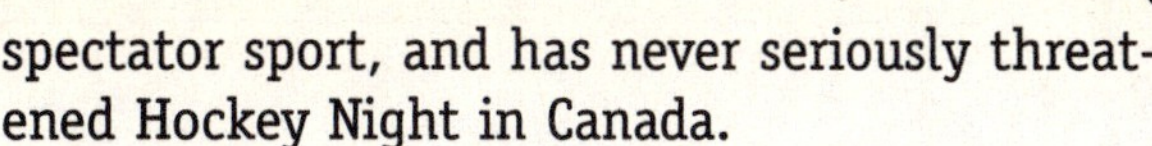

spectator sport, and has never seriously threatened Hockey Night in Canada.

Whatever their derivation, skis were adopted early on by alpine troops, who developed the skills needed for several James Bond movies. Military skiing was in fact so demanding that it pretty well eliminated fighting as part of battle. Thanks to its ski brigades, Sweden has remained neutral during several world wars. The soldiers were so fully occupied by skiing and firing a rifle at the same time that it seemed impractical to involve them in further conflict. Today, ski troops are used mostly to trigger avalanches, which make no territorial demands beyond burying tourists.

As for civilian skiing, this did not become a fully sexy pastime till 1904, when the Norwegians opened a skiing school in France for the French military. The French immediately saw that skiing was a kind of courting display, with all that this meant in the way of lucrative ski resorts in the French Alps. In no time at all, European royalty discovered the French ski spa as the ideal place to shed inhibitions without inflaming the mob. The exhilaration of the sport was augmented by excellent French wines and a shortage of oxygen that gave new meaning to "Your Highness."

Today, skiing reigns in all snow-blessed lands as *the* upscale way to incur a compound fracture. Skiing combines spiritual exaltation with the unique experience of being airlifted to hospital. How to invoke this midwinter night's dream is the stuff of the pages that follow.

642 A.D. Suddenly, skiing happened.

CHAPTER 2

How Fit is Enough!

Leg Lifts, Elbow Lifts and Forklifts

TO SKI, THINK BODY. It doesn't matter whether you are of sound mind. What counts on the hill is having the physical stamina of a musk-ox combined with the grace of a ballet dancer and the survival instinct of a lemming.

No need to take a commando-training course. Or steroids. Sheer bulk can actually be a drawback—in the gondola for instance. Other passengers will glare at you for testing the vehicle's load limit. You may be jettisoned. Embarrassing.

On the other hand, having *some* musculature is desirable for skiing. The sport will be more fun if the skier can ascend a flight of stairs without going on life support. Skiing with tubes in your nose and an IV-bag slung on a ski pole may be gutsy, but other skiers will find it depressing.

Similarly, if sitting in the balcony of your local theater causes you to black out from oxygen depletion, your lungs may not be ready for Whistler. No one expects you to be part Sherpa, breathing comfortably at 29,000 feet without a mask. But having to concentrate on inhaling and exhaling, rather than avoiding the mature pine in your path, can detract from enjoyment.

[Note: ski-store clerks cannot be relied on to give you an accurate assessment of your fitness to ski. So long as you are strong enough to carry a debt load, the store will overlook minor blemishes such as *rigor mortis.*]

Should older people take up skiing, and if so, how far? Skiing has been suggested as an alternative to the death tax. It is estimated that over a trillion dollars will be inherited by the adult children of today's seniors, many of whom persist in living despite the baby boomers' need for capital. This is why we hear them say, "You're never too old to ski!" and see wheelchair-accessible ski lifts. Which sell one-way tickets at a reduced rate for seniors.

But this should not discourage old folks—even over ninety—from engaging in this great sport. If you fit into this age category, simply keep in mind that your

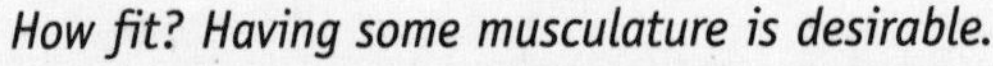

How fit? Having some musculature is desirable.

walking with two canes does not automatically qualify you for ski poles. And before you sign over a living will to a relative, you should check the document for a clause that authorizes your being entered in a Giant Slalom event.

If you are a child, how old do you need to be to learn to ski? This depends on the child. A *well-behaved* child can be taken skiing as early as four or five. But if the parents have a rotten, tantrum-throwing kid, it is reasonable to push him onto the slope at eighteen months. As a substitute for his learning to walk. The crib is readily attached to a snowboard.

Remember, in ancient times, female infants were left exposed on the mountainside to die. Today, there is gender equality. Male fry too can be put up for adoption by a she-wolf. Romulus and Remus on sticks.

Whatever your age, you can test your fitness for skiing by doing a simple exercise: *knee bends.* The basic posture of the skier being that of sitting on an invisible biffy, it is essential that you can bend at the knees. Don't be misled because people have told you that you know squat. Prove it to yourself.

Parents get nasty brats on the slopes quickly.

If for some reason your knees lock rigid or, worse, only bend backwards, your chances of winning a World Cup downhill are considerably reduced. But don't be discouraged if your knees have lost their flex. Maybe you just need new shocks. Possibly replacement of the entire suspension system. Your ski shop will be happy to refer you to a specialist.

Before you invest in expensive ski equipment, there are a few other fitness tests you should conduct on yourself:

1. Do you have a pulse? Almost a necessity. Despite appearances, skiing is a strenuous activity. If you think that Newton's law of gravity will do all the work on the downhill, you have let your applelike shape affect your judgment.

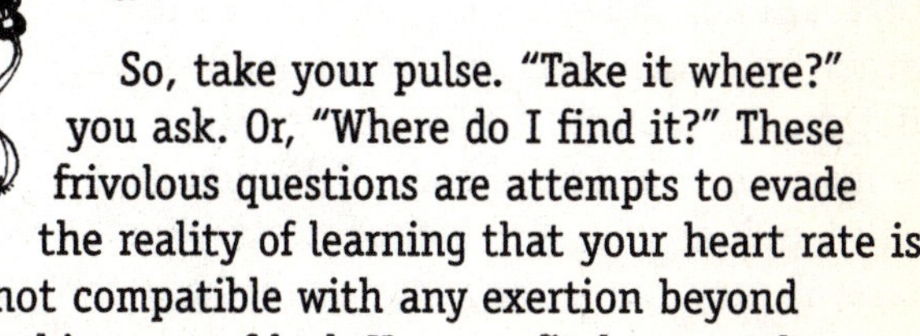

So, take your pulse. "Take it where?" you ask. Or, "Where do I find it?" These frivolous questions are attempts to evade the reality of learning that your heart rate is not compatible with any exertion beyond climbing out of bed. You *can* find your pulse without asking a police officer. It just takes a bit of patience.

Your pulse, if any, should be discernible:

a. between the tendons of your wrist. If your pulse is sixty beats per minute, what you have probably checked is your wristwatch. Only people who are very healthy have a resting pulse of sixty. *Your* resting pulse will almost certainly be higher than sixty because you get anxious about taking your pulse. Unless you can take your pulse by surprise, it will be 120 per minute or more. Especially if you take it:

b. on either side of your windpipe, just below your jaw. You have often seen TV drama doctors take a pulse this way before they say, "He's gone." If *you* think you have gone, or are about to go, grabbing yourself by the throat may give you a false reading.

You can ask someone else to take your pulse. Make it someone who has absolutely no emotional effect on you, like your accountant, your meter-reader, your spouse.

Assuming that you have found your pulse, and it doesn't sound like a Caribbean steel-drum band, what does it say about the readiness of your heart to accept some exercise? Do you have reason to believe that you can come to some agreement? Unless you have been exercising regularly, your heart will be astonished by the sudden demands that skiing puts on circulation. Then it gets miffed. "I was never consulted" is the last message your brain receives from your heart before it takes you to court.

2. Do you have quadriceps? Almost as requisite as a robust rear. Quadriceps are not found in a Jurassic Park. Yours may have fossilized, but more likely they just need toning up.

The quads are located in your legs. That is, between your fanny and your feet. This is the section of your body that is most involved in total skiing, though you can also use it for other functions, such as remaining upright. But on the ski hill, flabby quads can jeopardize your entire body. Other skiers will laugh at you, and kick slush in your face, if they sense that your quads have the tensile strength of tapioca.

Never mind the upper body. You won't be using it except to top off your legs. Cross-country skiers *may* want to work on their arms to ward off nearsighted birds of prey, but if you don't plan to use your ski poles for much besides pointing out the route to the restroom, bulging biceps are purely decorative.

So, start your exercise program *pianissimo*. Unless it is against your religion, try walking. Slowly at first. Work up to a stroll.

Then, after you have ambled a block or two, stop and take your pulse. Don't be surprised if a fire engine roars up, siren blaring, and paramedics jump out to clap you onto a stretcher and initiate CPR. It just means that one of your neighbors has seen you standing on the corner, clutching your throat and mouthing the count, and has called 911.

Be grateful. If walking a block has accelerated your pulse to 210, you are either ten years old or about to suffer cardiac arrest. To clear this up, try to engage the medics in conversation till your pulse has dropped back down to a number closer to your age.

Walking, swimming, cycling—none of these vigorous pre-ski activities should be begun without the warm-up exercises that identify the pro who has learned to put off the actual hard labor as long as possible. Stretch each major muscle group. Slowly and sensuously. If you don't have enough major muscles to make a group, *don't fret*. Just keep stretching what you've got, languorously, till someone comes up to you and says, "I say, I couldn't help admiring your gluteus minimus . . ."

In this regard, believable buns are critical. For both sexes the tush is the basis of first impression. This is why ski pants are made to fit snugly. They have to send a clear message through a blizzard. The skier may have dimpled knees, lush body hair, seductive ears, but these features are lost under outerwear.

Another reason to beef up your bottom: studies show that the novice skier spends 90 percent of his time falling on his butt. Putting a pillow in your pants is an unattractive hindsight.

Concentrate on your quads. Do *leg lifts*. [Note: these should not be confused with the quad lift that is a type of aerial ride with seating for four. You shouldn't need three other people to complete your quad lift at the fitness center or in the discomfort of your own home. There you simply lie on your back or stomach and use your legs to pump iron till you question the meaning of life.]

These *repetitions,* as they are called, will teach you to count in a new way: "One, two, three, six, nine, twelve . . ." It is a form of exponential math, possibly invented by Einstein while he was pushing weights, in the same way that he condensed time by riding a stationary bike.

Organized repetitions are called *power sets.* You are not permitted to break up a set. Should the power be cut off, find a floor mat and lie there doing toe-ups. If questioned, explain that you consider strong toes to be the most underrated factor in winning a Super Grand Slalom.

Allergic to the smell of other people's sweat? You can skip the fitness center and crank up your quads by simply walking down stairs. Take the elevator to the top, then walk down to the main floor. This works the same leg muscles you will use for braking and impacting objects on your skis. It may, however, draw stares if you do it repeatedly at the office. After the receptionist has seen you emerge from the elevator for the fifth time in succession, without ever taking it down, it could be all she needs to trigger a nervous breakdown.

On the plus side, if you break your leg walking down stairs, friends will still be happy to sign their names on your leg cast, and you have cut out the middleman of costly ski resorts.

For balance, walk a floor beam at the gym or any handy construction site. Walking a railway track is not recommended, whether or not you have a drinking problem.

During the off-season (summer and autumn), instead of playing tennis or golf, or doing something else that you risk enjoying, *speed-hike up a mountain.* Take your Alpine ski poles and agitate your arms as though this were relevant. Then, after you get to the top of the mountain, *run down the mountain.* Carrying a weighted backpack. The steeper the decline the better. Ignore ordinary hikers who yell, "Where's the forest fire?" Repeat this drill till you are picketed by Greenpeace.

Practice yoga for flexibility. Sit on the floor. From the lotus position, entwine your arms and legs till you look like a meditative pretzel. *Do not try this when alone.* You may need help disengaging yourself. Assistance from two or more people. The aim is to become flexible enough to be able to wrap your legs around the back of your head because that is the position you will be in after your first downhill.

In order to ski effectively, you must be pliable in body and mind. This is why very young children can make you look foolish on the slopes and should be avoided. Should you find yourself in a beginners' class with a child under ten years of age, push the kid into the path of a snowcat as soon as possible. You don't need the aggravation.

CHAPTER 3

How Rich is Enough!

Ski Gear and Your Piggy Bank

THE THREE major investments that a person makes in a lifetime are:

1. Buying a home.
2. Buying a car.
3. Taking up skiing.

Thinking that you can do all three is ridiculous. You may be able to swing the condo and the coupe, but adding the cost of skiing—gear, garb, ambulance, rehab, wheelchair, course in basket weaving—is beyond any but Colombian drug lords. Who will vouch that, in the mountains, the most difficult pass to negotiate is the ski pass.

This explains the sport's unique contribution to our social structure: the ski bum. No other form of recreation causes the adherent not only to forego all worldly goods but to make the hegira to Aspen on a charter flight that mortifies the flesh. There is no such thing as a golf bum. Manic though golfers' devotion may be, they rarely give up a normal family life entirely in order to pursue the perfect fairway.

That understood, what are the items that the novice skier must put his savings into instead of a registered retirement plan? Which should he buy first—the ski clothes, the skis or the Calvin Klein Eau de Skint? Let us assume that the skis have priority, since it is theoretically possible to ski in the nude.

The Skis. Unless you have unusually long, skinny feet with upturned toes, skis are required for skiing.

Now, skis are sold in pairs. Ski-shop clerks will not look kindly on your asking, "Can I buy just one ski to see if I like it?" It doesn't matter that you are a one-legged person, though you may escape with a tongue-lashing. Either you buy both skis or you buy a snowboard. Snowboarding is an entirely different activity, too vulgar to be discussed in this section.

Skis are made of wood. Judging by the price, the wood comes from a tree so rare that it has disappeared from all parts of the known universe and has to be grown in secret biospheres run by Swiss gnomes.

What length of ski should you buy? As a rule of thumb, the longer the ski, the shorter the skier's life-span.

Visiting a ski shop is the beginning of your financial slide.

Reason: You go faster on skis that project beyond the toe of the boot. Short skis are therefore safer, but may be mistaken for Persian slippers.

Many ski texts provide graphs to correlate the length of the ski with the height and weight of the user, as well as your hat size and political affiliation (if any). For instance, you should hesitate to buy skis fourteen feet long if your height is under three feet. Midgets are certainly entitled to compete in ski races, but unless they weigh over 300 pounds, using the longer competition skis is apt to increase their insurance premiums.

Conversely, if you are over seven feet tall, your using twelve-inch skis will be seen as reluctance to engage in any skiing event that involves movement.

Actually, the safest place to wear skis is on your shoulder. In the ski store. Study yourself in the store's mirror, carrying the skis in a sporty manner. Observe whether the skis keep slipping off your shoulder, which would indicate that your shoulders are too narrow for skiing and perhaps you should be thinking croquet.

[Note, too, that quality skis come with a binding strong enough to hold the ski boots after the owner has taken leave of both. The ski harness differs from the horse harness in that it is of no help when you yell, "Whoa!" The first loyalty of the ski binding is to the ski.

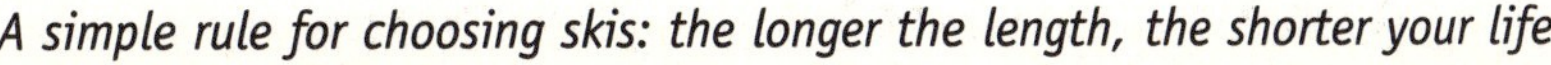

A simple rule for choosing skis: the longer the length, the shorter your life.

Regardless of the unplanned trajectory of the skier, a good binding stays with the skis right to the bottom of the run.]

How much should you pay for your skis? If you are a beginner, you may be wise to buy a pair of previously owned skis, sold as part of the estate of the deceased.

Skis advertised in *Buy and Sell* can be a real bargain and perfectly serviceable once the blood has been scrubbed off. But be wary of ordering skis from the TV Home Shopping Channel.

An early attempt at safety: Issac McDiesel's steam-powered safety bindings, ca 1928. McDiesel was unable to solve the problem of the tiny lines freezing, and eventually abandoned the concept.

Another early safety binding: Gretel and Hans Yodelstern's Swiss Clock Spring Binding, ca 1938. A proven system, its one major drawback was the enormous key the skier had to carry to rewind the mechanism each time it was sprung.

Wilbur Ott's Rocket-assisted Ski Bindings were tried once by the inventor in 1963. Ott was last seen in 1963.

Skis that are delivered in a compact cardboard box, and that need to be assembled with the aid of instructions written by an alien with delusions of ESL, rarely prove satisfactory.

For this reason, most people take the trouble to personally shop for their skis in a shop that specializes in this form of extortion. And since you will be mortgaging your home to pay for your skis, you ought to *try them on.* Yes, right in the shop. As if they were extra-large sneakers. Just be prepared for a bit of an adventure. You will be actually applying the skis to your feet with the help of a clerk whom you may have to marry after all the clutching and grabbing.

Whatever price you pay, you should expect your skis to come with a lifetime warranty, or three weeks, whichever comes first. Also, roadside assistance. Except in Norway, automobile associations do not recognize skis as a vehicle. But for the kind of money you're paying, the manufacturer should pledge to have someone come and rescue you from a ditch if no one else will touch you.

[Note: it *is* possible to rent skis at the ski facility "for the day, week or month." Choose the day. Make it an hour if they are prepared to haggle. With the chances of your surviving longer on rented skis being ultraslim, why waste the money?]

The Ski Poles. You ask: "Do I really need ski poles?" Answer: Yes. Ski poles give you something to hang onto besides an orthodox religion. Without ski poles, your hands have nothing to do and are liable to get into mischief. Making obscene gestures at other skiers. Picking your nose or where your nose was.

The poles also help to maintain balance for people with arms shorter than the average orangutan's. It is false economy to buy expensive skis and then try to make do with a couple of old broomsticks with a nail on the end. First impressions are important in social skiing, and having an extended toilet plunger tucked under each arm presents a negative image.

[Note: for cross-country skiing you may need a ten-foot pole, normally used not to touch things with.]

The Ski Boots. Very, very pricey. These are the Bentleys of the boot world. But the skiing novice should reject the idea of buying a pair of used boots from Army Surplus. Such boots may be cheaper and more durable, but they simply lack the spacious aspect of detached housing for the feet. The proper ski boot has several feet per square foot and is sold by a Realtor. The old lady who lived in a shoe would have killed for a ski boot, having enough room upstairs for eight more children.

Since you will be selling your mother into slavery to pay for your ski boots, you should test them in the shop. Wearing ski socks. Your feet will find the ski boots intimidating enough without having to cower there naked.

Also, you ought to be able to attach the ski boot to the ski without using scotch tape. The system of straps and buckles is complicated and may require extra study by a person who has not learned to tie his shoelaces.

As a rule of thumb (or toe) you should not choose ski boots that, individually, weigh more than you do. Your ski boots will be of only marginal use if you are unable to lift them out of the trunk of your car. Some skiers try to get around this problem by never removing their ski boots once they get them on. One might think that this would complicate their sex life, but most insist that being permanently ski-booted actually adds to sexual pleasure, though hard on bed sheets.

The Ski Suit. Entire fashion shows are devoted to style in skiwear, and would be seen on TV if the models were more perceptibly braless. Yet your garb should be close-fitting. Aerodynamically, flappy clothes that catch the wind on the downhill run can render the skier airborne without a pilot's license. You do *not* want to billow. There are better ways of scaring off other large animals than appearing larger than you are.

Also, snug duds can function as a primary sexual attraction, unless you have a shape best clad in a muumuu. Studies show that the average recreational skier spends only 10 percent of his or her time actually skiing at the ski facility. The rest, and obviously most, of the skier's time is spent bending over to adjust something—a maneuver in which correctly fitting pants are critical to the success of the declination—or ascending a barstool, reclining decoratively on a stretcher or otherwise presenting a beguiling body profile to observers.

Colors? Ski clothes should be bright—red, orange, fluorescent—to be more possibly visible to aircraft searching the mountain canyons for your body. White is definitely out. Yes, everyone does seem to love Frosty the Snowman, but that is not reason enough for you to adopt the coloration of a shroud.

To be seen is more important than to be admired. If you can find a ski toque topped with a red flasher, like an emergency vehicle, buy it. Klaxon siren optional.

[Note: buying a jumpsuit does not commit you to jumping. Jumping is, or should be, sheer joyous impulse regardless of what the skier is wearing.]

The Ski Underwear. Very important. Even though you wear nothing else skiing, wear underwear. The first thing that first-aid attendants do is strip off your outerwear. You may be on television for the first and last time. You don't want to be remembered by thousands of viewers as "that poor slob in the trapdoor skivvies." Thermal underwear, yes. You should strive to avoid hypothermia as long as possible. But giving up pretty lingerie—particularly if you are a woman—can chill the libido that makes skiing so vital to the baby food industry. You may have to search a bit to find a ski store that sells fur-lined bikini briefs.

Whatever your choice, be sure to own more than one suit of thermal knickers. The skier is apt to perspire freely, and after a couple of days on the slopes wearing the same Stanfields, he may find that he is asked to ride the gondola on the outside.

The Ski Gloves. These should have fingers. Ten, minimum. Some skiers try to cut costs by wearing mittens that Grandma knitted instead of springing for a real birthday present. But mitts compromise both your grip on the ski poles and communication with the snowboarder who has just sprayed snow in your face. Denied the eloquence of the middle finger, the skier is tempted to open his mouth, freezing his gums before the teeth are extracted.

The Ski Helmet. Worn by a beginner, a helmet will be viewed as somewhat pretentious. The helmet is associated with a high level of competition, as is wearing a bib with a number front and back. The beginner who affects these accessories before he has learned to stand on the skis may find them a dubious attention-getting device.

If, on the other hand, you desire to wear a ski helmet to conceal a receding hairline or really heavy drifts of dandruff, go ahead. It is possible to buy an all-purpose helmet that can be worn for skiing, biking, sky-jumping and meeting in-laws.

The Ski Goggles. More impressive than mere shades, goggles protect the eyes from sun glare and flying objects such as small children. Welder's goggles will not do. For the compleat skier, it is essential that the goggles or sunglasses be of the mirrored type that identifies you as a celebrity who doesn't want to be identified.

Wearing glasses that allow strangers to see your eyes in a naked face is bound to attract no interest whatever. Mystery is a major factor in glamour. With proper accessories, you can intrigue bystanders without ever leaving the ski rack. Indeed, learning to ski becomes redundant. If your purpose is to get a sex life, however briefly, the key is static skiing in attractive apparel. After all, it *is* hard to enjoy intercourse wearing a neck brace.

Crutches and/or Cane. Buying a prosthesis before you attempt skiing is a rather negative approach to the sport. You will have ample time to buy or rent your crutches after you are discharged from the hospital. It is better not to tempt fate beyond wearing a wristband bearing your name and the phone number of next of kin.

Accident insurance. Like earthquake insurance, ski-accident insurance is not easy to buy. In fact, if you ask for it, most insurance agents fall about in fits of laughter, possibly injuring themselves and suing you. More practical is to buy a good used prayer mat. Watch for garage sales on the east side.

CHAPTER 4

Ski School

The ABC of Ski and the Tic-tac-toe of Snow

NEARLY EVERYONE should take ski lessons, unless, of course, what they want to learn is how to play the flute.

But ski instruction is really useless unless the learner is strongly inclined. To an angle of forty-five degrees. It is no asset to be addicted to verticality. You must be able to bend when bidden. You need to have the Right Stuff. If you insist on your mother's accompanying you to ski school, at least don't hold her hand.

Some skiers are self-taught. This means that their instructor was an idiot. Most of these learned to ski as young adults who happened to find a set of skis on top of someone's parked car. They improved their chances of discovery by hanging around a ski facility parking lot.

But *no one* should try to learn to ski unaccompanied by at least one other person. That person need not be a priest, though that would be comforting. But the companion should be physically strong enough to extract a large object from the branches of a tree without having to call in the mountain rescue team. It is too early in your skiing career to use up the goodwill of those volunteers who will later have to extract you from the same tree.

Should you let some other member of your family teach you to ski? This depends on whether that relative has reason to believe that he or she is remembered in your will. We all know that, when learning to drive a car, it can be a serious mistake to take instruction from our dad. Especially in this era of stepfathers. Even granddad can be lethal. The family member who becomes severely irritated with us for repeatedly mistaking the accelerator for the brake is liable to become even more abusive when we keep spiking his foot with our ski pole. In short, it may be false economy to save money on ski lessons if it costs you the love of someone who otherwise might be sorry to see you die.

How, then, does one find a professional ski instructor? Unlike other escort services, ski instructors are not listed in the Yellow Pages. What *are* advertised are ski schools. Ski schools are not regulated by the Department of Education. The only thing they fall under is an avalanche. Not being publicly funded, the ski school may not provide a free lunch or separate washrooms for boys and girls.

Ski school is the only school where pupils go *inside* at recess.

Since ski schools are usually run in connection with ski resorts, the learner should expect to have to pay for his lessons. Possibly with his life. So, before registering for a ski school, check on the success rate of its graduates. Are any of them still alive? Do not be influenced by class photos—smiling students clustered around their instructor. The art of embalming is very sophisticated today, and a casket is by no means needed to provide the violently deceased with a better color and longer fingernails than before they took the skiing course.

Beware of any ski school which:

1. calls itself First Memorial Ski School, Roselawn Ski School or the like. The

school is probably run in conjunction with a funeral home. Try to avoid doubt that what happens to you on the training slope is an accident.

2. asks you to sign an organ-donor release form. Again, the hint of subcontracting invites caution.

3. makes you wear a large L on your back during lessons. Just because you are a learner is no reason for you to be humiliated. The ski instructor who enforces discipline by making the student eat snow or stand on one ski for an hour may be just striving for a Dickensian atmosphere. Alternatively, he could be a gelid psychopath.

4. is overly permissive. Dewey principles of education do not work any better in the ski school than in any other elementary school. Don't let yourself be deceived by a teacher's report that described your getting sucked into a snow-making machine as a form of self-expression. The ski instructor who makes no mention of physics, the force of gravity, or the dynamics involved when an irresistible force collides with an immovable object, is almost as dangerous to the student's well-being as a Home Ec teacher.

Does one need to learn to speak Chinese before taking ski lessons? In her definitive work on the subject, *The Centered Skier,* author Denise McCluggage (this is a real name) assures the reader that it is not necessary to know Chinese so long as one grasps the principles of *t'ai chi. T'ai chi* teaches how to relax without losing tension . . . how to make falling a positive experience . . . how to combine *yin* and *yang* with *up* and *down,* not to mention sideways.

While the benefits of seeing skiing as an Oriental approach to life (and probably death) are manifest, *t'ai chi* should perhaps be thought of as a supplement to nonmetaphysical instruction rather than as a substitute for sheer terror. The fact that there are to date few notable Chinese skiers in sports annals indicates that meditation while hurtling down a hill at sixty mph is not conducive to a protracted career.

Whether or not you enlist in ski classes, you should be familiar with the steps of learning, which have increasing degrees of impossibility. The first step being:

Putting on Your Skis. This is best done in the privacy of your own home, assuming that your home has at least one room larger than a bread box. If you are living in an abandoned piano crate or tenting in the park, you may have to go outdoors to find space enough to master the art of attaching ski to boot. Since this could expose you to the scrutiny of neighbors or bystanders (a crowd could gather), you should be prepared to hear derisive laughter, thigh-slapping and remarks such as "Better stick to slippers, Clyde."

Ignore them. As your Mom told you: pay no attention and they will go away. Also, there is a safety factor in having someone present when you try to put on your skis. There have been unfortunate cases of persons being attracted to a house or apartment by a strong smell, and on entering discovering a partly decomposed body still attached to skis put on backwards.

If it is impossible for you to be monitored, at least place a telephone on the floor within crawling distance of where the assembly is to be attempted. Then:

1. be sure you are wearing your ski boots *before* you put on your skis.

2. put on your ski boots according to the manual. If you don't understand instructions printed in a Nordic language, take care to open the top of each boot wide enough to admit your whole foot. This could take some time. Do it sitting down, preferably on a futon that can also serve as a bed or bier.

Be sure that your foot understands the difference between the *inner* boot—the part that cuts off circulation—and the *outer* boot, whose weight will surprise everything below your hips.

3. When you have reason to believe that your foot is completely immersed in the boot, do up the buckles. In the correct order. Middle buckle first. This is harder if your boot has only two buckles. A one-buckle boot is hardly worth doing up at all. It is going to fall off your foot the first time you cross your legs.

The multibuckled boot, however, affords an opportunity for you to make so many refined adjustments, snugging the foot ever more firmly into the boot without creating anxiety in the ankles, that it will be too late to go skiing that day at all. This is how a really expensive ski boot helps to prevent leg injuries. The less time you have left to actually ski, thanks to your state-of-the-arch boots, the better your chances of delaying admission to the orthopedic ward.

When you have your boots firmly buckled, walk around for no less than ten minutes to let your feet settle. This extended walkabout indoors gives you an opportunity to note any discomfort, such as people living downstairs coming up and kicking you in the shin . . .

One, two, buckle my shoe.
Three, four, walk no more . . .

Moral: You should have taken a hike in the ski shop, where the clerk organizes boot customers into a platoon for close-order drill.

Having walked your boots, lie down on the floor and decide whether your boots feel equally snug all over (good) or are causing what is technically known as pinching your foot (bad). *This requires exquisite judgment.* Delay taking drugs. Once your boots are properly fitted, you may start drinking. Heavily if your feet hurt.

Finally—and this is a delicate subject in our era of gender angst—it is necessary to understand that some ski boots are made for men, others for women. This sounds sexist, and the

Better ski schools come fully equipped to make your learning experience the most rewarding.

authors apologize for raising the matter in a work intended to avoid controversy unless it will help to flog the book.

However, the strictly anatomical fact is that ski boots sit differently on the skis because men tend to be *bowlegged,* women *knock-kneed.* This is not to imply that women don't have the right—hard fought for—to be as bowlegged as men. As indeed some women are, especially after age ninety. And, of course, a man may be knock-kneed without indicating anything about his sexual orientation.

So, whether male or female or undecided, you should study your legs in a mirror. Are they an O or an X? This is not an idle game of tic-tac-toe. If your legs show gender bias, you may need to supplement your boots with *cant-plates,* wedge-shaped pieces of metal that compensate for your being built like a rodeo clown. Otherwise, you will be skiing on only the edges of your skis—very fast, but terminal.

4. Attach your boots to the ski binding. This will take care of the rest of your weekend.

Reason: The binding is the trickiest part of the whole boot and ski assembly! There are spacecraft that have fewer delicate adjustments than a ski binding. Unless you have a degree in mechanical engineering, it may be simpler to just affix the ski with an old jockstrap or, if female, a stout garter belt.

But assuming that you have bought skis that have a binding, you ought to try to understand the purpose of this hardware in an ideal world: *To prevent you from hurting yourself when you fall.*

This is, of course, a visionary concept in the same class as the chastity belt. Which it somewhat resembles. Except, in putting your foot in it, you make a serious commitment.

Examine your ski binding. You will find that it consists of a *toepiece* and a *heelpiece,* which you can think of as a bear trap. Your boot is the bear, lured into the trap by the smell of fear. The toepiece (foreboot) consists of a release-setting indicator, an antifriction pad, a screw for adjusting the release-setting and a partridge in a pear tree.

The heelpiece (aprèsboot) is made up of the manual release, a screw for adjusting the release-setting, the ski brake and (optional) the cigarette lighter.

Before you start fiddling with all these adjusters, you must weigh yourself on scales that you can trust better than the ones you keep in your bathroom. The reason for this is that to comply with safety regulations set by the German Industrial Standards Association (DIN "Ve haf ways of making you safe."), the ski binding must conform, on a scale of one to ten, to the weight of the skier. For example, if you weigh twenty-two pounds, your DIN setting is one. As your weight goes up, so does your grade of binding till you hit ten (441 pounds). This is another good reason to watch what you eat. Putting on a lot of weight can put a strain not only on your heart but on your ski binding. Unless you keep buying stronger and stronger bindings, your big fat feet will simply shuck your skis, and you will roll down the hill as an enormous snowball, probably taking out a small village.

Before choosing a binding, you should also check the strength of your leg bone. If you have a flimsy femur, you need a weaker binding, since, all things considered, it is better to lose a ski than to break a leg. (This criterion may not be valid in Scotland.)

You can test your leg bone by using a pair of calipers to measure the width of the shin where it joins your bent knee. Do this in the ski shop and you will see why skiing has become so popular. Just buying the equipment can provide more fleshly delights than are found in some English marriages.

All these measures are designed to assure that, under stress, your ski will disengage before your leg does. Don't be afraid to err on the side of caution, so that your skis fall off if you sneeze. Become too married to your skis and you can face a messy divorce.

5. Ski brakes or ski straps? Yes, you have a choice of accessories. Most bindings come with ski brakes designed to stop your skis from hurtling down the hill after your feet pop out of the bindings and your skis are free, free, free! It is possible to buy ski bindings with ABS. These will stop your skis on a dime while *you* go hurtling down the hill, confident that your investment is secure.

Less expensive are ski straps, which tie your skis to your legs. The disadvantage of ski straps is that if your skis fly off your feet with force, the whirling skis may create a helicopter effect. Becoming an impromptu chopper is not everyone's first choice as an exhilarating adventure.

CHAPTER 5

Getting it On

Skis First, then Boots or What?

WAXING. Skis are of two kinds: waxable or waxless. Waxless skis are for beginners who want to stay that way, and alive. These skis are nothing to boast about. You may not even want to take them out of their ski bag. Especially if your ski bag is a converted golf bag your uncle left you in his will.

What waxless skis say about you is: "I don't want to go too fast because my body is a temple and demolition is not in my plans." They are best suited to night skiing, when there is less chance of people's noticing that you are not moving.

But even though your skis are bare boards whose base has the slickness of Velcro, you need to know waxes and waxing. Studies show that 90 percent of resort lounge conversation is devoted to wax. To be wax-illiterate is social ruin.

Consider: ski waxing is a science in itself. People who go on to post-graduate work at ski school write doctoral theses with titles like "The Influence of Kick Wax on U.S. Foreign Policy."

For other skiers, waxing is an art. They wax poetic . . .

Sublime, the climb,
the gliding, sliding ecstasy
of subtly waxéd skis . . .

For all, ski waxing has a mystique. Some skiers become so engrossed in this ritual that they never make it to the run. By the time they have their skis waxed entirely to their satisfaction, in accordance with predicted weather conditions, the snow condition and the back condition they've developed from waxing their skis, the season is over.

How, then, do you gain the expertise required to rate as a wax-skier *par excellence?* First, accept the fact that you don't qualify just because you have waxed your car. Not unless your car rides on the roof much of the time. Nor does floor waxing permit you to skip a grade. That bottle of acrylic polish, applied to your skis, could draw the wrath of Friggin, the Norse goddess of Slush.

No, you must buy the whole kit of ski waxes, complete with the authorized version of application, and an altar on which to kneel while administering to the golden bough. You will note:

The Holy Wax Chart. This lists the proper, color-coded wax to apply at certain temperatures and for specific snow. Viz:

Snow Temperature	New Snow	Mature Snow
14 to 30°F	Green	Blue
30 to 32°F	Blue	Violet
Above 32°F	Red	Yellow

You will see at once that you are in trouble if you:

1. don't have a snow thermometer, or
2. you are color-blind.

Before applying the wax, you must thoroughly clean the base of your skis with an approved solvent, removing burrs, fibers and stool. (Deer can be dirty.)

Next, iron your wax. If you have ever had to iron your shirt, it still won't help you to iron your ski wax. You can, however, use a standard clothing iron if you don't happen to own a waxing iron. A curling iron is fine for making wavy wax, skis with a perm, but don't do it near a window where neighbors can see you.

A No. 9 iron, while best for getting your wax out of a sand trap, has likely got into your ski bag by mistake.

When your wax has stopped smoking and the emergency vehicles have returned to the firehall, allow the wax to cool. Then scrape it all off. For this you need an authorized scraper. Your fingernails may do a reasonable job of removing your ear wax, but if you break a nail it affects your après ski.

Make sure there is no wax left in the grooves, rills and other valleys of your ski base. Unless you floss your skis after every waxing, they will develop gum disease.

After you have spent the productive years of your life waxing your skis, you may find that you have applied the wrong kind of wax—grip wax for Alpine skiing or kick wax for cross-country—presenting you with an alternative: change the kind of skiing you want to do or throw away your skis and start all over again.

Despite this rather demanding ritual, ski waxing is essential to the skier who needs an excuse for:

1. coming last in a race.
2. falling down in the lounge.
3. breaking up with a spouse.

Wax is the Rocky Mountain scapegoat. Without it, you have no one to blame but yourself—a vile smear.

Adjusting to Outdoor Skiing. The student of skiing will find conditions to be quite different when she or he leaves the house and goes to the actual mountain. Putting on the skis, for instance, takes on an added dimension of unfeasibility. The same operation on a hill that is not as user-friendly as your bedroom can be an aerobic exercise in frustration.

Reason: the presence of snow. Perhaps you anticipated that your learning to ski would involve contact with this form of precipitation. But it is not till you are actually up the mountain, and having trouble remaining upright before you even get your skis off your car's ski rack, that the reality of snow begins to sink in.

For one thing, snow is much more slippery in person than it appears on TV. It will be of no assistance when you try to put on your skis outdoors. This is why it is advisable to do it in a secluded spot. Like behind an abandoned cabin. (You may have to wait till it has been abandoned.)

Assuming that you have found a flat place out of the public eye, yet still in the same mountain range, here are the steps for putting skis onto boots in snow:

Step 1. Knock the excess snow off Boot #1. You can use your ski pole for this snow-cleaning, though you will be standing on one leg, which some people find to cause nausea. If you have a history of one-legged motion sickness, take a Gravol and wait for thirty minutes.

Step 2. After you have removed the excess snow from Boot #1 and are standing on one leg, look for your skis. In a perfect world, they would be lying handy, side by side, with the brakes on. More often, however, they will, for reasons known only to skis, have moved away from you for distances up to a mile. Retrieve them from their new locale and repeat Step 1.

Step 3. Place snow-free Boot #1 into the binding and spend a moment in contemplation of how you will remove the excess snow from Boot #2. Ski manuals recommend using the edge of Boot #1's binding to scrape the bottom of Boot #2, while you lean on the ski poles. Known as the *faux pas de deux,* this maneuver requires extraordinary balance. If the semicircular canals of your inner ear have frozen over, despite your earmuffs, you will topple over. Repeat Step 1.

You see? It is entirely possible to spend your whole ski holiday trying to get your boots into the binding while standing in snow. This is why skiing is so dangerous: you can become a slobbering mental case right there in the parking lot. So, do try to be accompanied by someone willing to clean the snow off your boots for a reasonable hourly rate so that you can progress to the stage of actually wearing skis when you fall down.

Among your childhood fairy tales, you may have heard the one about the magician who put on his skis while standing on a slope. Even some skiing manuals say that this is possible.

Putting on your skis will afford many interesting opportunities to meet new companions.

Don't believe it. Not unless you have one leg shorter than the other. (It may be worth measuring. There is an outside chance that you are related to the legendary sidehill gouger—the creature adapted to running along the mountainside and becoming extinct when it tried to reverse directions.)

"Stamp out a ledge or platform in the snow, so that the skis will not slide away when you put them on . . . ."

Visionary. Pure moonshine. The workers who groom the ski slope can become very surly about novices who go about stamping ledges or platforms in their snow. Because when other skiers careering down the slope hit your ledge or platform, they lose the fillings in their teeth. They may find this irritating. You could find yourself wearing your skis up your nose.

The other hazard in donning your skis on a slope is that if you forget to apply the brake, your ski will take off down the hill on its own. It then becomes a Cruise missile, seeking out any target big enough to beat the sh-t out of you. The best you can hope for is that your runaway ski will fly into a ravine, never to be seen again. You can then dispose quietly of the remaining ski with a brief burial ceremony, return to your car and compose the story about how you had your skis stolen while you were in the washroom.

What are the odds against your ever being able to take off your skis once on? Slim and nil. It may be easier to simply live with your skis on, though it means taking up permanent residence on a mountain. Of course, should you have no intention of ever skiing again—because, say, of an unexpected return to sanity—it is reasonable to at least *try* to take off your skis. Because binding-release mechanisms vary—some pulling up, some pushing down and still others refusing to budge without an explosive charge—you should not count on being free of your skis this side of Doomsday.

[Caution: Do not let frustration make you resort to lower-limb amputation. There *are* orthopedic surgeons who will perform a skiectomy, for a fee, but they tend not to mention side effects, such as compromising your tango.]

Skis on, you are now ready to stand on them, if only to have your photo taken. The first thing you will notice at this elevation is that your ski boots are built to cant you forward, whether or not that is your best profile. You will be better prepared for this if you normally wear high heels (a realtor or cowboy). Otherwise, you likely will fall on your face—a position from which there can be no recovery. You can fall in practically any other direction and still eventually lead a normal life. But when you pitch forward, it's game over. Your efforts to regain the upright merely bury your face deeper into the snow, where suffocation makes further instruction unwarranted.

Remember those ski poles you were holding before you fell on your face? Each pole has a strap on the hilt to prevent your ski pole from slipping out of your hand, sliding down the slope and impaling another skier who has fallen on his face.

Next time, make sure the straps are wrapped tightly around your wrists. Before you lose all sensation in your fingers, grasp the ski poles firmly and hoist yourself erect. But not *too* erect. Standing tall may suit other outdoor activities, such as standing guard at Buckingham Palace, but in skiing, good posture is counterproductive.

Creative learners use any number of techniques to accustom themselves to the rigors of skiing.

Bend! Bend *everything.* When you are standing on your skis, there shouldn't be an unbent bone in your body. Your elbows are bent, your knees are bent, your ankles are bent.

Above all, *relax.* Relaxing is emphasized in every ski school as absolutely essential to all phases of mastering the boards, from the first erection to the final descent in the air ambulance. Entire texts have been written on how to relax when skiing. In fact you may wish to reconsider learning to ski if:

1. you grind your teeth in your sleep.
2. you smoke more than one cigarette at a time.
3. your analyst has described you as "anally retentive."

However, in our best-case scenario, you are now standing on your skis, properly bent in the right places. Now make sure that your weight is evenly distributed, as the manual says, "on the balls of your feet." How do you find the balls of your feet? What if your feet don't have balls? Wimpy feet? Some people have this problem. Duck-footed folk may be better suited to aquatic sports.

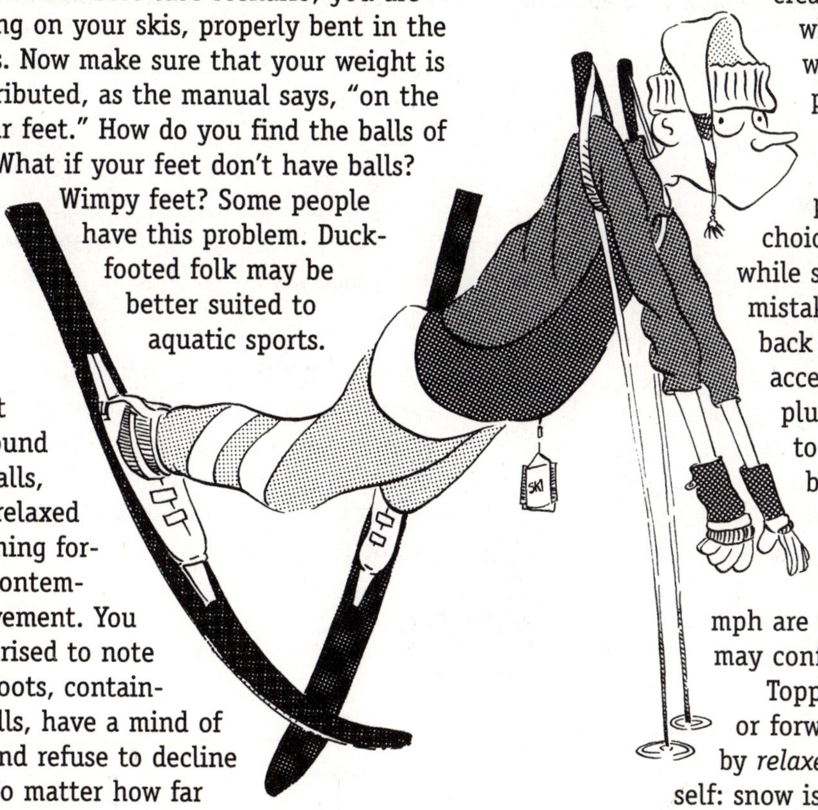

But let's assume that you have found your foot balls, are totally relaxed and are leaning forward as if contemplating movement. You will be surprised to note that your boots, containing your balls, have a mind of their own and refuse to decline with you. No matter how far you lean forward, your boots remain unmoved. You can slope forward till your nose is almost touching the ground—pretending you are a ski jumper in midflight—but for the fact that your Achilles tendons have snapped like uncooked spaghetti.

[Note: any skiing posture that results in emergency surgery, a leg cast and six weeks on crutches must be considered flawed.]

You are now ready to learn how to fall. Believe it: in skiing, falling is nothing to be ashamed of. The slopes are packed with fallen women and quite a few men of questionable descent. *Everyone* falls on skis. Professional skiers fall all the time without disgrace. The only thing that distinguishes their falling from your falling is that they get up afterwards.

The point is, the experienced skier falls *deliberately*. It is part of his skiing technique. Experience has taught him or her that falling is the best method of stopping in an emergency, much superior to ramming a tree or Renfrew of the Mounted.

If you have time, you can even declare, in a loud, clear voice, "I THINK I'LL FALL NOW." This alerts skiers behind you that you are about to create an obstacle over which they themselves will fall—a guilt-free pileup of bodies.

What is the best way to fall on purpose? The natural choice is to fall backwards, while stifling a scream. A mistake. Falling onto the back of your skis merely accelerates your downward plunge. The opportunity to gaze up at a clear blue sky is offset by your suddenly becoming a luge event, in which speeds of 100 mph are not uncommon. This may conflict with your plans.

Toppling stiffly backwards, or forwards, can be avoided by *relaxed* falling. Tell yourself: snow is not as hard as the pavement you are accustomed to falling on. Snow is soft. Cushiony. Especially fresh, deep snow. In fact, lying in the snow after you have fallen in it can be the most enjoyable part of your day's skiing. You can attach a red flag to your ski pole to warn other skiers, and just lie there making angels in the snow till removed by men in equally white suits.

However, you still need to fall correctly in the

first place if you are not to do yourself a mischief. All skiing texts advise: don't try to fight the fall. Once you are reasonably convinced that you are going to founder—because your sense of balance is screaming "May Day! May Day!"—resign yourself with grace into *the safe fall.* This proven method of falling consists of subsiding, as casually as possible, *sideways.* Hands up, you surrender unconditionally. Try to land on your ear (left or right ear, depending on the slope). It is almost impossible to sprain your ear. But falling on your hands, elbows or knees can incur injury requiring medical treatment more extensive than merely sewing your ear back on.

Theoretically, you will never break your leg falling because your boot will come out of the binding before the bone shatters. This is why it is important to check and adjust the release mechanism of the binding *before* you start to fall. As a fall-prone beginner, you ought not to have set the release so that your boot hangs onto your ski like grim death (the other option). Better to have a quick divorce than a long and painful relationship with your skis, for the sake of the children.

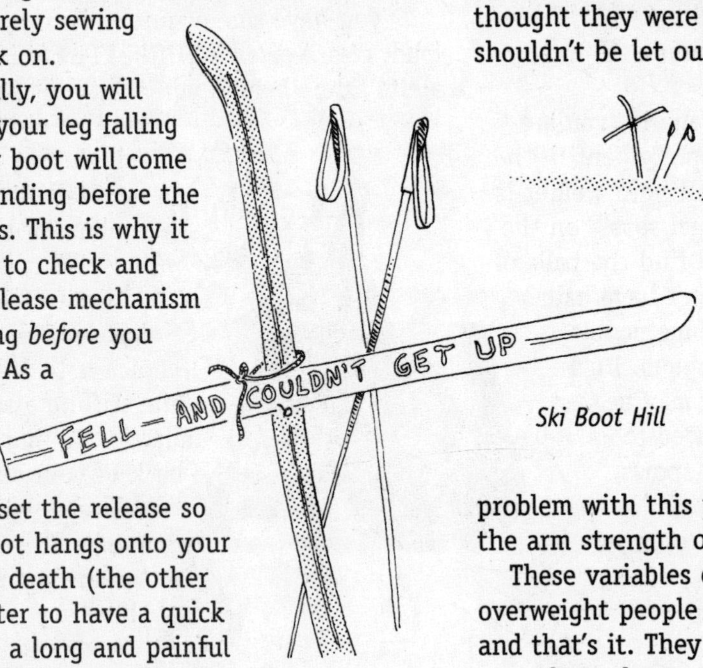

FELL—AND COULDN'T GET UP

How do you get up from a fall? Many ski instructors try to avoid answering this question. They understand, as indeed you should, that getting up from a fall is impossible. This is, literally, the downside of skiing. It is something not talked about at ski resorts because it is bad for business. The owners find it more practical just to cover up the fallen skiers with the snowblower and call it a new mogul run.

The only way to avoid being permanently fallen on the ski slope is to be accompanied by someone who cares enough about you to cope with a hysterical tangle of arms, legs and skis. *Don't count on a spouse.* It should be an easy decision for your companion whether to hoist you up or leave you to compost. Also preferable is that the person not be on skis, as your frantic grabbing at their arms and legs will precipitate them in turn. With both of you down and helpless, and darkness setting in, recrimination is likely to dominate the conversation—an ugly kind of double suicide.

Now, some ski manuals do exploit your credulity by suggesting a way that you may resume the upright position with assistance from whatever god you pray to. This scenario depends on your hands being still attached to your ski poles. If you left the poles in the washroom, or thought they were a barbecue utensil, you really shouldn't be let out of the house, let alone onto the ski slope.

Ski Boot Hill

Assuming, however, that the poles are strapped to your wrists, the theory is that you put the poles together, across the slope, and use them to lever yourself erect. The only problem with this procedure is that it requires the arm strength of a full-grown gorilla.

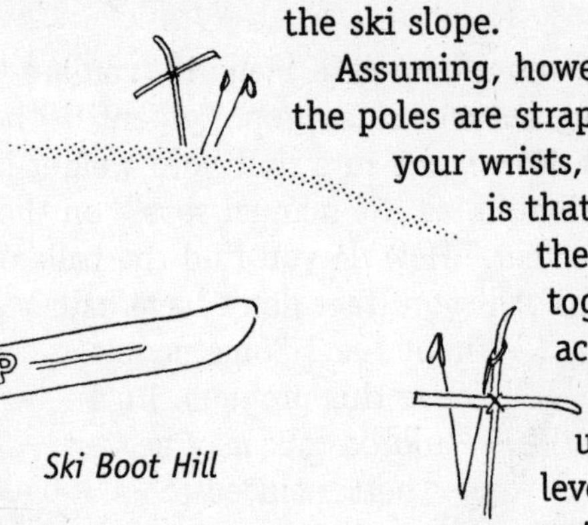

These variables explain why you never see overweight people skiing: they fall down once, and that's it. They have to be towed away, still recumbent, by tractor.

CHAPTER 6

Inclined for the Slopes!

Taking Your First Steps

SOME NOVICE SKIERS are not satisfied with a full day of falling. They have enough energy left to consider actually going up the hill. They sense that going up the hill is the only way that they can ski *down* the hill. How to get up there?

A privileged few may reach the top of the mountain by helicopter (see Chapter 9), but this is not character-building unless the chopper crashes. *You are not allowed to take the ski lift.* The ski lift is for experienced skiers. They know already how to walk uphill on their skis. They may even spit on you from a height as you trudge up the mountain. This is all part of your initiation as a skier. Yes, it *is* humiliating that you are also assigned to what is called the nursery slope. Don't be misled by the word *nursery*. Should you become unnerved enough to soil your diaper, there is no nurse on duty to change you.

How, then, do you struggle up the hill? The recommended moves are:

1. the Herringbone.
2. the Sidestep.
3. the Hokey-pokey. (This will not get you up the hill, but is a lot more fun.)

The Herringbone is so called because of the pattern your skis make in the snow before you slide backwards and fillet yourself. The movement consists of splaying the skis in opposite directions to fool the hill into thinking you don't know which way you want to go. You must also walk on the edges of your skis, while pushing firmly on your poles and smiling as though physical agony is your chosen lifestyle.

The Sidestep—only slightly less implausible than the Herringbone—consists of edging up the slope sideways, skis parallel, edges dug into the snow. It is like walking up stairs aslant, one step at a time, as you do at home after celebrating Robbie Burns Day. In fact, if you sprinkle a little snow on your stairs, climbing them sideways can be as emotionally satisfying as sidestepping Mont Blanc and a lot closer to your liquor cabinet.

Whichever method you choose, Herringbone or Sidestep, it may help to remember that having to walk up a mountain on skis has been condemned by Amnesty International as cruel and unnatural punishment.

Turning around on skis is a decision that should not be made lightly. If, for instance, you just want to see if you are being followed, it is simpler to attach a rearview mirror to your nose. Also wiser than trying to turn around is to make up your mind right at the start which direction you intend to go, and continue in that direction for the rest of the day. On most mountains this will eventually bring you back around to the point of departure, though it may take a few weeks. Pack a lunch.

However, if you are determined

The Herringbone

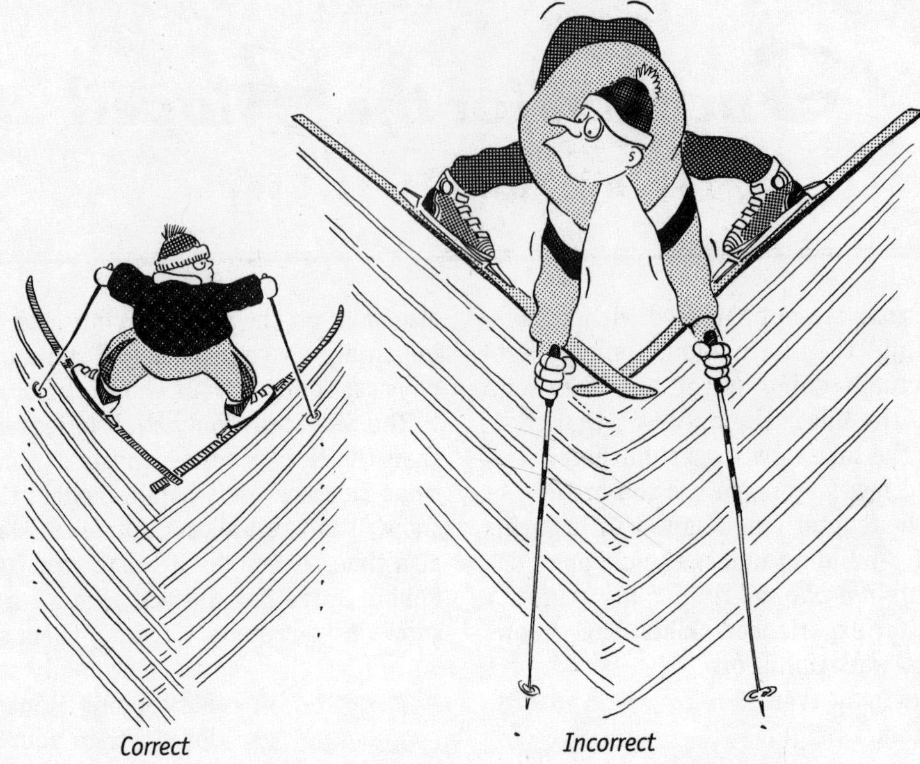

Correct

Incorrect

The Kick Turn

to turn around on skis because you are on some sort of imagined schedule, what you can try is:

1. the kick turn, or
2. the sidekick.

The kick turn, the usual method of trying to turn on skis, is nonetheless maniacal. The hypothesis is that you kick one leg high enough that the ski is perpendicular to the ground, while you take your weight on both ski poles and the other leg. If the tail of the upright ski gets stuck in the snow, you face the prospect of spending the rest of your life as a tripod.

To avoid this fate you must whip the airborne ski around ninety degrees and place it parallel to the other ski, but facing in the opposite direction. In normal ballet this movement is called the *entrechat.* In skiing it is called *dementia praecox.* The victim has visible evidence that he doesn't know whether he's coming or going. If he already suffers from chronic indecision or dual personality, the kick turn can be devastating.

As in tutu ballet, there are variations of the kick turn. The degree of difficulty depends on the length of your skis. Wearing *short* skis (one foot or less) will make it easier to swivel the ski around overhead without getting its tail trapped in the snow. But if your skis are long jobs—that you bought because the salesperson said, "On these babies you'll go like a bomb"—your kick turn will be like laying a quarter mile of railway track, no hands. And you will regret the speed lust if your boots, facing in opposite directions, take off with your skis, splitting you like a chicken bone before you can even make a wish.

Safer is the sidekick. The sidekick is a large friend who accompanies you on snowshoes wherever you go, and on request lifts you bodily, skis and all, and places you headed in the opposite direction.

Now, it follows that it is easier to develop the sidekick if you are a small, attractive woman, rather than a 200-pound male. If a sidekick is not available, you can rent one for the day. Try the bars at the ski resort. Realize that you could become emotionally involved with the sidekick. The buddy system of turning may not be for you if already married.

After attempting the kick turn or sidekick, you understand better why the ski manuals mutter, in small print, something about ". . . it helps to be a trained acrobat." Indeed it does. Spending a couple of years with the Ringling Brothers Circus, as a member of the Flying Spinozas, would not be amiss.

[Note: *not* recommended is the *high kick,* which consists of taking a flask of rum from your pocket and applying it to your mouth till you forget why you wanted to turn.]

The Sidekick

Skiing downhill—at last, the moment you have been working so hard to enjoy! Your reward for having to put on your boots and skis, for learning how to fall, turn and curse in languages you didn't know you knew!

Skiing straight down the hill is called *schussing* or, if you have difficulty with Germanic tongues, *straight running. Schuss* is the German word for "shot." It is better not to think about this too much. Just enjoy the word as a vigorous spray of saliva.

Schussing presumes that you have somehow managed to reach the top of what is called the fall line—an unfortunate choice of words, but then ski parlance tends to be brutal. (Another name that may give you trouble is that for the groomed run, namely *piste.* How you pronounce *piste* can affect how you impress other guests at the ski lodge. The correct pronunciation is "peesed," to rhyme with "deceased.")

Now, how do you make your straight run down the fall line? First, *don't look down.* At anything. Don't look down the hill. Don't look down at your skis. Don't look down at the mouth for having got yourself into this life-threatening situation. Gaze straight ahead, while trying to see as little as possible. Closing your eyes entirely, however, is not advised unless you are a very strong believer in transcendental meditation as the way to schuss.

Your skis should be placed neatly parallel to each other, your weight equally distributed. *Don't look down at them!* Let your feet tell you whether you have placed one ski on top of the other—a sandwich that will disagree with you. Beginners often ask—in their trauma-recovery class—"How far apart should my skis be if I ever try to schuss again?" The stock answer: your stance should be as wide as your hips. This means that if your skis are more than three feet apart, you should be engaged in child birth, not skiing. Or, if you find that your skis are snugged against each other—DON'T LOOK DOWN!—you are hipless. You now know why people call you "Snake."

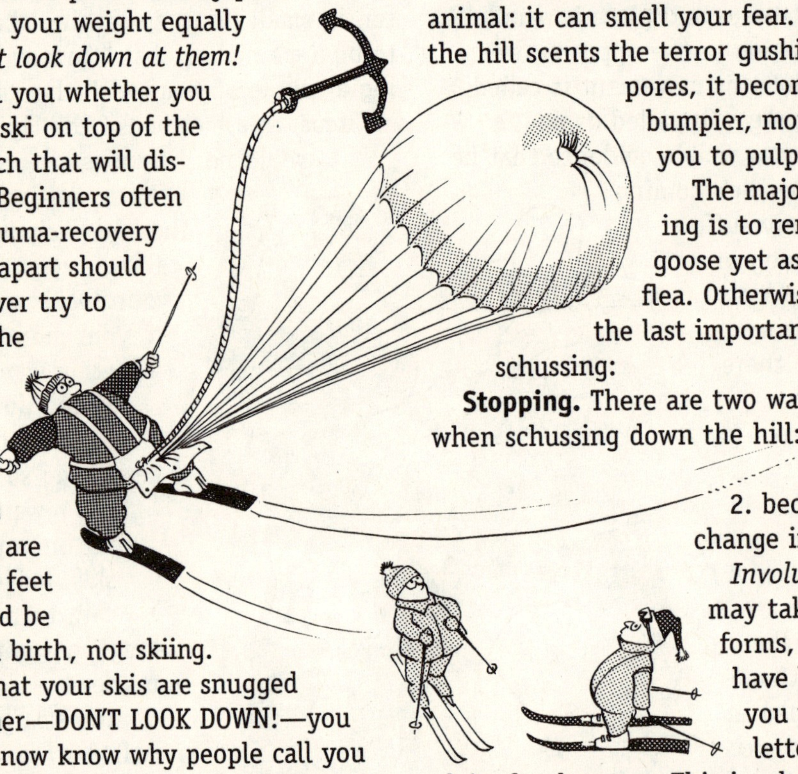

Don't fret about your hips. Right now you need to be totally relaxed. Let your shoulders hang loose. Flex your legs limply. Let your ski poles dangle behind you, as though confident that neither will be needed to splint your broken leg. Bend your knees and ankles just a tad, as though you are about to sit down on something till you notice there is no toilet paper. Above all, *don't lean too far forward.* You will be hurtling down the fall line soon enough. Having your head arrive first will earn you no extra points.

Now you are ready to push off down the fall line. Try not to tense up. One skiing expert (Denise McCluggage) suggests that you think of your precipitation as "grooving with gravity." This Zen approach to schussing depends on your being able to picture Buddha barreling downhill at sixty mph.

Above all, *do not yield to panic.* Panic will freeze you into a rigid projectile with survival prospects of a meteor. How can you tell when you are panicking? One telltale sign is when you hear someone screaming, with an interesting echo effect from neighboring mountains, and realize that it is you.

Remember, the fall line is like any other wild animal: it can smell your fear. And the instant the hill scents the terror gushing from your pores, it becomes steeper, bumpier, more eager to reduce you to pulp.

The major challenge in skiing is to remain as loose as a goose yet as nimble as a sand flea. Otherwise you will blow the last important element of schussing:

Stopping. There are two ways of stopping when schussing down the hill:

1. on purpose, and
2. because of a sudden change in plans.

Involuntary stopping may take several different forms, most of which have lawyers from whom you will be receiving a letter outlining the claim for damages. This is why you really should not be schussing for the first time if there is anyone else on the slope or indeed in the same county. Ski, if possible, during the off-peak hours between midnight and 5:00 A.M. They are called *off-peak* because that is where you will go unless you have a miner's lamp strapped to your forehead. Most ski resorts turn off the lights after 2400 hours, so you will need to choose a night with a full moon. Skiing by moonlight can be the thrill of a lifetime, cut short though that may be.

Voluntary stopping on the slope is more complicated than simply running into another skier/fence/tourist bus by accident. The commonest technique is called *snowplowing.* Snowplowing comes naturally to skiers from the prairies. They have seen lots of plows—the farm variety—and understand the principle on which the device works. In contrast, skiers from large urban centers think of the snowplow as a city works truck equipped with a blade that piles the snow into their driveway. They expect to have to scatter rock salt behind them—counterproductive when snowplowing on the ski slope.

But as a braking system in skiing, snowplowing does not involve participation by municipal works crews. You must do it with the equipment at hand (or foot).

The trick is to tuck the toes of your skis together to create a V, while standing on the edges of both skis so they bite the snow. Since this maneuver requires your doing two things at one time, you should practice on flat terrain. Persons who have difficulty simultaneously patting the top of their head while rubbing their stomach ought to respect that limitation and do all their skiing in Saskatchewan.

Obviously, snowplowing is easier if you are pigeon-toed. But it is hardly worth having surgery to correct feet that are not attracted to each other. Besides, you have another option for stopping on purpose:

Falling. In skiing, retardant falling is defined as "allowing the entire body to come into contact with the snow as soon as possible." This subsidence should sooner or later arrest your descent, though the distance covered on your chin depends on the steepness of the hill. If it takes longer than ten minutes to stop after you have fallen, you have somehow strayed from the nursery slope onto the White Hell slope. As soon as you are able to talk, ask the medics. You don't want to repeat that error, should you ever be well enough to resume skiing.

Learn to recognize the ski-run symbols before making your way to the top.

Ski-slope Symbols

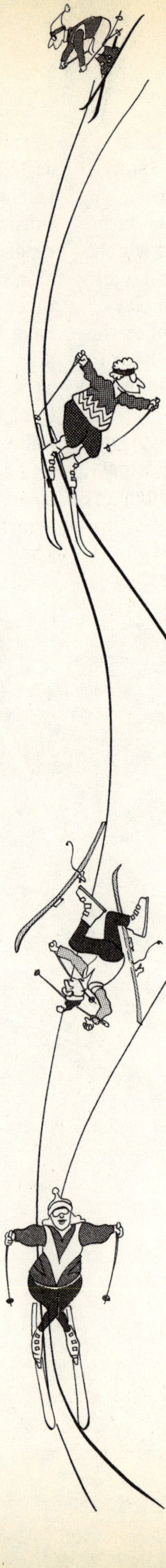

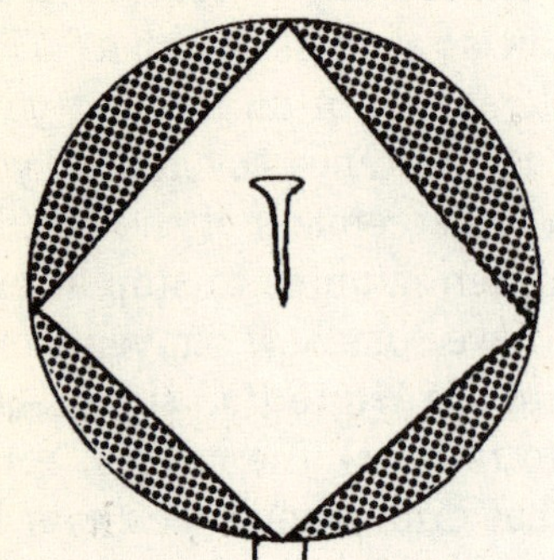

Green Diamond – replace your divots.

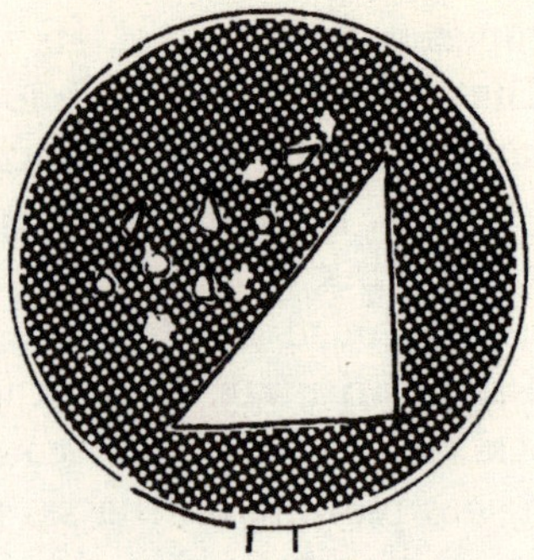

Avalanche Zone – no yodelling.

Bunny Slope – safe for all.

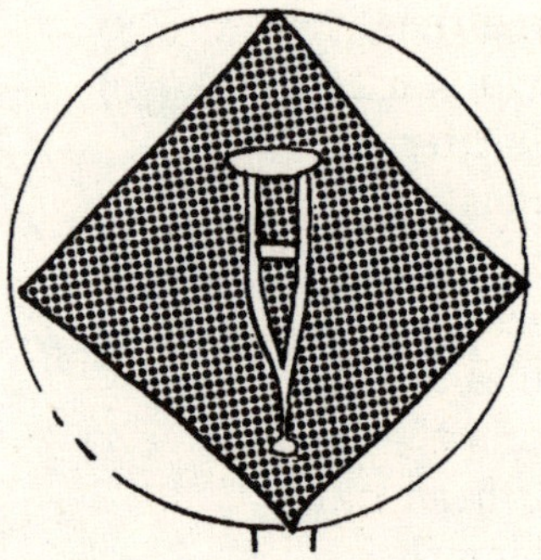

Red Diamond – check your insurance.

Truckers – check brakes.

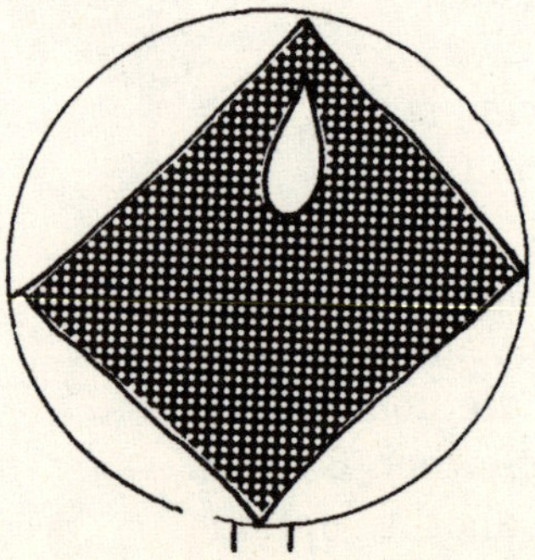

Black Diamond – don't cry for me, Argentina.

CHAPTER 7

Done to a Turn

Going Round the Bend

WATCHING recreational skiers on TV, you must have noticed that they derive much of their euphoria from zigzagging down the fall line. This illustrates a basic geometric principle: *In skiing, a straight line is the dullest distance between two points.*

Much as you may consider it a triumph that you have reached the bottom of the hill with only your stomach being turned, you should aspire to:

Traversing. Sounds like a kind of sexual aberration. But in fact it is possible to traverse a slope without sexual arousal of any sort, unless going sideways really turns you on.

Traversing shows the hill that you have a mind of your own. You are *not* going to schuss straight down the hill. You are going to toy with it. By moving *across* the fall line! (Not *too* far across or you will be off the slope and into the woods to be lost forever, giving the hill the last laugh.)

Traversing depends on *body angulation*. In order to put more weight on one ski, you have to angulate your body into what is called the *banana position*. Just wearing a yellow jumpsuit will not cut it as a ski Chiquita. Unless you can bend in the middle, the closest you will get to the traverse position is a banana split.

Don't push your Schuss.

But with proper body angulation, you can switchback down the slope, making the run last longer, along with your life. Indeed it is possible to spend the whole day slowly zigging and zagging, putting off having to walk up the hill again. Safer yet, you can remain at the top of the hill, bending your banana into the traverse position, while someone takes your photo. No one needs to know that you were not moving and had no intention of moving when the picture was taken.

Stemming is impossible to explain without using one's hands. Also known as the half-plow, the stem requires turning outward the tail of one ski, angulating your banana and wishing you had stuck with the rumba lessons. It gives you a fresh insight into your muscular coordination. Don't be too disappointed if you discover that you have the reflexes of a broken flywheel. There are other no-turn types of skiing that you can enjoy, such as cross-country in Siberia, where you can ski for thousands of miles without having to turn or stop once.

Sideslipping is much easier than stemming. You don't need to be in an airplane to sideslip. All you have to do is stand sideways on the slope, without digging in your skis, and sneeze. You then slide slowly sideways down the hill, yodeling merrily to show other skiers that your line of descent is illegitimate.

Skating. For skiers who make a fetish of actually moving on skis, skating is an option. Especially if you have skated on ice, or rollerbladed, or lived with a slippery bathroom floor. The technique is the same:

Step 1. Push off from one foot, whichever you trust more.

Step 2. Glide forward on one ski, while throwing forward the opposite arm and shoulder in the direction you hope to skate, while humming "The Skaters' Waltz."

Step 3. Repeat this alternating thrust of legs and arms till you detect some movement forward. (If you find that you are skating *backwards,* let no facial expression indicate that this is anything but your intended direction, calling for a very special skill.)

Some people have a problem with swinging the left leg forward with the right arm, or the right leg with the left arm. This is no bother if one is a horse, qualifying as either a trotter or a pacer. But skiing does not lend itself to harness racing. So, if you suspect that you have this odd disorder of the motor center of the brain, have someone watch you walking. If the person reports that you swing the right leg with the right arm, while closing the right eye, your locomotion is dominated by the left hemisphere of the brain, and you probably walk in circles a lot.

If so, forget skating on skis. To skate, it is essential that your legs find the courage to move independently from your arms. Sure, you hate to threaten them with sock suspenders or something. But without skating you have zero acceleration on skis. You may as well hook yourself up to camp utilities and rent yourself out as a trailer.

The pleasure of skiing illustrates the old proverb "One good turn deserves another." The skier gets his rush from making an S of himself. Or, less compulsively, herself. The

buzz is especially strong when the curving descent is carved in fresh, deep snow where no S has gone before. With virginity so little prized in other venues of life, the skier's assault on a pristine slope is a rare treat with little risk of being arrested for molesting a minor. Not only are most mountains millions of years old, but they are able to renew the chastity of their snowpack every winter. Thus, the passionate skier may rip the blanket at will.

Step-Turning. This daring move calls for lifting one ski, while in motion, and putting it down at a different angle from the ski that is wondering where it went. Exquisite timing is required to transfer the weight at the crucial moment to avoid subdividing a torso that you would prefer

to keep unspoiled. You must overcome the natural tendency to keep both skis in contact with the snow, and content with remaining parallel, till someone tells you that the ski season is over.

But step-turning must he mastered in order to proceed to:

Jump-Turning. Here both skis are lifted aloft, simultaneously, with your body twisting quickly enough to provide for some chiropractor's old age.

People who have jump-turned down the fall line insist that it is just about the most fun you can have at a ski resort without going inside, and that they intend to repeat the thrill as soon as the pins are removed from their ankles.

Short-Swinging. Does not refer to intervals of sexual promiscuity. But there is some connection between short swinging and swing music, in that both depend on a sense of rhythm bordering on the supernatural. To check on yours: did you never play the drums as a child? Do you think of a Newfie fiddler as a type of crab? Associate rhythm with a method of birth control? If so, you may have a problem with swinging, short or long, on skis.

For instance, you will be unable to graduate to the slalom race (see Chapter 8). You will be limited to the straight and narrow, which many skiers regard as a sign of frigidity. Unable to look back and see the graceful curves you have cut in the snow, you may even become resentful and bitter, deliberately running down small children on the nursery slope to which you are confined, in perpetuity, because of your robotic locomotion.

Can nothing be done to improve one's sense of rhythm? Besides, that is, watching old Elvis Presley movies? Some people swear by Chinese herbal remedies, such as ginseng and shark's prostate. They claim that these Oriental potions have improved their syncopated flexion, liberated their hips and enabled them to rotate their knees without the assistance of a metronome. However, these remedies have not been clinically tested in actual skiing conditions by volunteers who have not mixed them with alcohol.

Jumping. This is an attention-getting device said to be an excellent source of adrenaline. Because jumping on skis is a form of heavier-than-air flight, however, it should not be attempted till you have completed your estate planning.

Terrain jumping. Is not to be confused with jump jumping (see Chapter 8), which is even more likely to end sadly. Terrain jumping is how you cope with casual bumps on the slope.

Question: Is it okay to jump over a fallen skier prostrate in the snow?

Answer: Yes, so long as you are convinced that he or she is unconscious.

The formula: the bigger the bump, the higher the jump. Really *large* bumps are called mountains and should not be jumped without a parachute. A rather *small* bump is called a mogul, which sounds like a powerful business executive but probably isn't unless there is an expensive cigar jutting out of the snow. Moguls are man-made for freestyle skiing competitions (see Chapter 8), so if you encounter a lot of them you are likely on the wrong course and should fire a flare.

But ordinary terrain jumping—used for routine bumps, fences, ridges, bridges, etc.—requires no turning, no sense of rhythm, in fact no sense of any kind. What you *do* need is legs that can serve as *shock absorbers.* If you have ever watched a Boeing 747 land on the runway, you may have noticed the puff of smoke as the plane's wheels absorb the impact of all that weight. Whether or not *your* knees smoke, they should have a comparable capacity to spare you a pancake landing and consequent hip replacement.

To improve your chances of performing the terrain jump without permanent physical disability, practice the *tuck position* of midair suspension. For this, you draw the knees up to the chest and lean forward in an aggressive crouch—i.e., much the same posture as if you were flying economy class with a Mexican airline. *Attack* the bump. Hate it! Think of the bump as your mother-in-law. And don't lose your nerve. When you are airborne is no time to change your mind about jumping, let alone to review your past life. Regardless of how high your bump has suddenly proved to be—ten feet, twenty feet, Empire State Building—*stay cool.* Remember, we all have to go sometime . . . .

CHAPTER 8

Competitive Skiing

Or, Hello ICU!

WHY WOULD ANYONE who aspires to being in their right mind choose to ski competitively? Where does the urge to compete come from when half the time the competitors can't even see one another for the blizzard?

Auto racing, yes. Understandable. It's a natural transition from driving in rush-hour traffic to competing in the demolition derby. And tennis players are of necessity competitive, since one would look pretty silly running around the court alone, playing against oneself. Similarly, track-and-field events lend themselves to competition. Entering a footrace is not odd for the person who has lived in an apartment building with only one bathroom. Golf, a gregarious game, encourages competition without the hazards of a contact sport, unless the ball is actually struck.

But skiing? Those who study the metaphysical aspect of athletics classify skiing as a basically spiritual experience. Like breaker surfing. Devotees of both surfing and skiing travel the world in search of the perfect wave, the ideal, pristine slope. No one tours the globe in a quest for the nonpareil Ping-Pong table, the supreme squash court. In such games, competition is of the essence. Running a marathon, too, is pointless done alone, without thousands of other marathoners vying for the honor of collapsing first at the finish line.

But skiing? Being alone with the wilderness winter wonderland is what skiing is supposed to be all about, at least till the happy hour. Competition may be rampant in the ski resort bar, where both sexes are vying for mates. But before you let that testosterone loose on the fall line, ask yourself:

Am I surrendering to male aggression disguised as sport? Am I shussing amuck as a surrogate for joining a SWAT team? Even though I am a woman? Betraying the feminist goal of eliminating competition, found guilty of contributing to male violence, domestic abuse and murderous orthodontists' bills for repair of minor-hockey mayhem?

Television is, of course, to blame. Young people see competitive skiing events on the haunted aquarium, the World Cup, where winning is glamorized by presentation of gold, silver and bronze medals, and they become podium-addicted. Especially if your son is a bit on the short side—face it, a dwarf—he will crave that chance to stand taller, on a box, and be handed a bouquet of flowers by an attractive young woman.

Regrettably, young women too are tempted into competitive skiing. Yet, just by meeting her at your AA meeting, there is no way of telling that a woman is a competitive skier. The way she crosses her legs—nothing to indicate that they are intimately involved with skis. It can therefore come as a shock to the young man just starting ski lessons to learn that the woman he is dating is known and feared by habitués of Grindelwald as "La Bomba." For this reason there is much to be said for remaining celibate, at least till you have mastered putting on your ski boots.

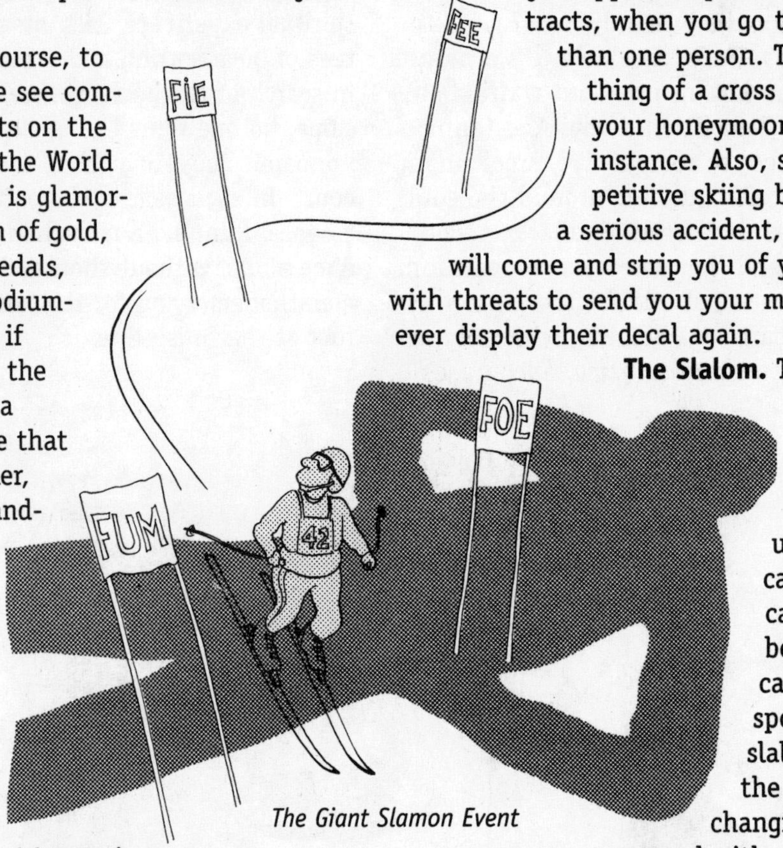

For both sexes, the lure of competitive skiing is as a way to get into advertising. As a moving billboard. After you reach a certain level of competition and are noticed by the sports media, all your equipment and clothing expenses will be paid by manufacturers to whom your body is a virtual reality TV commercial. Should you become a champion and still able to control the muscles used for smiling, you can make millions of dollars by endorsing products. What you actually enjoy endorsing is the checks.

The downside of sponsorship is that you must carry your name-brand, designer skis any time you appear in public or, in some contracts, when you go to bed with more than one person. This can be something of a cross to bear—on your honeymoon in Hawaii for instance. Also, should your competitive skiing be terminated by a serious accident, sponsors' agents will come and strip you of your jumpsuit, with threats to send you your mother's ear if you ever display their decal again.

The Giant Slamon Event

The Slalom. The slalom is a competitive event popular with skiers who have a natural talent for careering. And careening. Some become career careeners. One can spot the potential slalomer driving on the freeway and changing lanes at top speed without signaling. The four slalom events are:

1. the Special Slalom.
2. the Giant Slalom.
3. the Super G(iant) Slalom.
4. the Slalom and Gomorrah (an indoor event).

The Special Slalom is for competitors who have chickened out of the Giant Slalom. They still have to do the twisty-turny stuff, but at a slower speed than if they were on a real hill.

The object is to descend through a series of

gates. These gates differ from ordinary, garden-variety gates in that they aren't there. That is, the gate is just an open space between two poles, each with a flag on it. If the flagged poles are a fair distance apart, the slalomer is skiing on a golf course. He should get off the course as quickly as possible, since greenskeepers can be touchy about interlopers.

So long as you are on a proper course, the layout of which has been officially approved by the Federation International Ski (FIS), and okayed by someone wearing a large price tag on his jacket, you may assume that you are engaged in the slalom. The point of which is the same as when you are overdrawn at the bank: *You are buying time by cutting corners.*

The slalom is in fact described as "a race against the clock." This may be why the Swiss are so good at it. They know clocks better than anybody. Very few timepieces have reflexes sharp enough to keep up with a human being, even one who falls down a lot.

It is possible to have a slalom race without a watch by having the racers ski down two or more separate slalom runs at the same time. But this requires posting twice as many flags, and the organizers usually say the hell with it and retire to a pub.

The Giant Shalom Event

These people have enough to do during a one-course slalom race just dealing with gate-crashers. The slalom is one social occasion where gate-crashing is permitted, so long as you knock things over in the correct order. But the racer needs to remember that the advent of spring-loaded poles has changed the consequences of running into one of them at high speed. The effect can be much the same as that of stepping on a rake.

The Giant Slalom. The main difference between the Giant Slalom and the Special Slalom is that you have twice as many poles to run into. Also, instead of a single flexible pole topped by a red or blue flag, you have *two* flexible poles joined by two flags whose colors won't matter because you made the mistake of trying to salute them.

The Super G Slalom, as the name suggests, is the ultimate in dodging disaster. It is usually reserved for Italians or other persons who have lived a full life and want to weave their way into eternity.

This event is so fast that the slalom racer is apt to contravene one of the FIS regulations, namely "If the racer misses a gate, receives assistance or does not finish on at least one ski, he is disqualified from the race." It is hard to imagine a racer finishing the race on less than one ski. But the existence of the rule indicates that there have been slalom races in which a skiless racer crossed the line on the seat of his pants *and won.* Hence the prohibition against belly-whopping, back-siding or avalanching your way to victory.

The gatekeepers—judges posted at gates down the course—are also on the watch to make sure that "each skier passes with both feet through every gate." Now, it is hard to imagine how a racer could pass through without having both feet on the same side of the pole. Or, if male, that he would not sing tenor castrato for the rest of his life. But apparently some people will sacrifice a lot in order to save time.

These slalom-race rules result in fewer racers finishing the race than in other disciplines, such as pie-eating. Same as championship figure skating, one tumble can negate hundreds of hours of practice, neglect of family and job, and having to buy Absorbine Jr. by the carton. For this reason,

before you consider slalom racing, with its high potential for crushing disappointment, you should review your personality traits for evidence of suicidal tendency:

1. Do you become moody and have episodes of uncontrollable weeping after you find that you have put your slippers on the wrong feet?

2. Is walking into a closed door enough to discourage you from leaving your bedroom at all?

3. Are you subject to fits of acute depression triggered by minor mishaps like dropping your doughnut in your coffee . . . trying to light a paper match . . . the death of a relative who owes you less than ten dollars?

If so, you should opt for competitive skiing better suited to manic depression, namely:

Downhill Racing. In the downhill, the racer who falls feels less disappointment. In fact he likely feels nothing at all, being comatose. The reason for this is that the downhill is more keyed to speed, up to 90 mph. The importance of pace is shown by the fact that becoming airborne—flying over a large bump—can cost the racer precious hundredths of a second. Like a fat lady undressing, the more you take off, the less chance of having a good time.

Unfortunately, at the high speeds of the downhill race, a mishap can have more serious medical consequences than, say, falling out of bed. A recent downhill racing season, for example, was notable for the fact that 20 percent of the world's top racers were in hospital recovering from bad falls. This shows that, though the course is lined with bales of straw, there are better ways of having fun in the hay.

Watch some World Cup downhills on TV. Pay special attention to the slow-motion replay of a racer cartwheeling, skis splayed, into the fence net, there to lie with a total loss of interest in current events. Then consider whether it has always been your ambition to wear a body cast in a hospital where everyone speaks German.

Still game? Okay, what else do you need to downhill, besides the history of idiocy in your family? Very essential: to maximize speed, you must be *aerodynamically designed*. Here's how:

1. Your one-piece, NASA-approved suit must fit snugly, from neck to ankles, so as to create minimum wind resistance. Having large breasts may be a problem, especially in the male downhill. Also, you can forget about going to the bathroom for any reason other than to shave your beard.

2. You use extra-long skis. How long? Longer than your body, when laid beside you in the ambulance. The skis are also weighted to provide the acceleration of a scalded cat. But you should not presume that by using twenty-foot skis you improve your chance of reaching the finish line in a winning time. FIS regulations are firm about disqualifying the downhiller whose skis are longer than the course.

3. Your ski poles are bent to tuck into your body shape. You can either buy bent poles or use straight poles till you run into a tree.

4. Finally, if your ears stick out despite your streamlined helmet, you might think about having them clipped. Go to a qualified vet.

Regarding technique, downhill racing calls for a unique body posture called the *egg*. To simulate the egg, you crouch down on your skis with everything pulled in—hands, arms, neck, genitalia—to create the perfect ovum. Over which the air flows unimpeded. In World Cup downhills, the racer is egged on by spectators yelling, "Go! Go! Go!"—resulting in a scrambled egg.

Assuming the egg position.

In a typical downhill, the racer will descend a vertical drop of 3,500 feet in a little over two minutes. While this is slower than jumping off a tall building, you may be disconcerted by the salvo of ear-popping and possibly a nosebleed all over your egg. Test yourself. If after descending in the express elevator of a modern office building, you find that your hair has turned white and your nails are broken from trying to claw open the elevator door, you are perhaps not quite ready for Lauberhorn, Badgastein or even your local park playground's children's chute.

Ski Jumping. Ski jumping originated in Norway many years ago, when a sobriety-challenged skier inadvertently skied off the edge of a cliff, landed safely on his skis on the snow below, and instead of going to church to thank God for a lucky escape from death, went back and did it again.

He then persuaded some friends to join him in this aerial lunacy to see who could jump the farthest while yodeling, "O lady who!" This was the start of population control in Norway. Even today, there is no overcrowding in Scandinavia, unless one leaves the city and stands under a ski jump.

Ski jumping is without doubt the most spectacular of the Nordic competitive events, a sort of refrigerated rocket launch. Watching the Winter Olympics on TV, you can judge for yourself the comparative challenge of ski jumping or being shot out of a cannon. You will be impressed by the gracefulness of the top ski jumper soaring through the air like a prehistoric pterodactyl bent on becoming extinct.

Keep in mind: this competitive sport gives new meaning to jumping to a conclusion.

You should note, too, that the ski jumper's equipment does not include a parachute. The jumper also dispenses

with the ski poles. You may wonder what to do with your hands. Putting them over your eyes—not a bad idea, at first blush—is in practice not feasible. Instead, your hands should be parked behind your back, as you assume the egg position for the initial phase of the jump:

1. The inrun. The point of no return. Once you start hurtling down the two parallel ruts that some sadist has channeled in the icy ramp of the tower, it is too late to reconsider your mode of transport. You are committed. Your only option is to gain enough speed to avoid just dropping off the end like a stone, maybe damaging spectators.

2. The takeoff. This takeoff is no harmless impersonation of Elvis. The degree of difficulty is higher. You have to break out of your egg quickly, extending your legs to propel your body forward, as though you really intend to go where you're headed. Your nose is now in conjunction with the tips of your skis. There is no smoking during takeoff.

3. The flight. This should be the most graceful part of your ski jump, so stop screaming. Lean *way, way* forward into the wind to reduce air resistance. Imagine that you are a soaring bald eagle that has left the nest a tad too soon. Do *not* flap your arms. Bad form. The judges will deduct points for flapping, for trying to circle for a landing or laying your egg in a tree.

4. The landing and outrun. One certainty in ski jumping is that sooner or later you are going to land. Failure to land means that you have been caught in an updraft of phenomenal strength and will be reassigned to a balloon race.

Normally, however, you can focus your attention on *how* you make the transition from free flight to rather dramatic return to earth. Here, style is everything. You must absorb the shock of landing with the grace of a ballet dancer completing an *entrechat,* except of course you don't twiddle your feet. Remember, you are still wearing your skis, however briefly. Your arms are outstretched for balance, your skis poised one slightly ahead of the other in what is called the telemark position, after the Norwegian town of Telemark, which is famous for its positions.

The last stage of the ski jump is the outrun. This is when you get to stop. Not stopping is a boo-boo likely to alienate spectators gathered at the end of the run with the understanding that they will not be disemboweled by a jumper whose brakes have failed.

Almost as important as stopping is that you do so with a flourish, not losing your balance, falling over or yelling, "Oh, God, we're all going to die!" Judges deduct points for style faults. The climactic, graceful swirl . . . the raising of the goggles to the bronzed brow . . . the quiet smile of gratification at the mark posted by the judges—these are the signs of the master ski

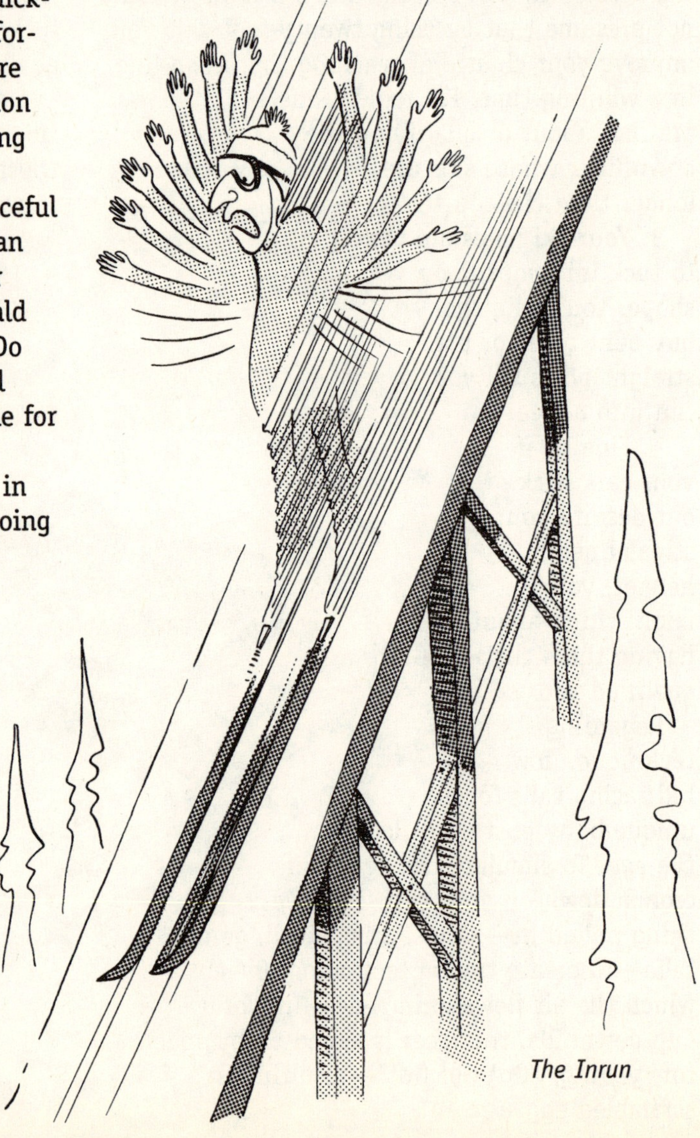

The Inrun

jumper. He does *not* stick out his tongue at the next contestant waiting to jump, give the judges the finger or otherwise display questionable sportsmanship.

[In regard to being a good sport, it is worth remembering that the most beloved ski jumper of all time was an Englishman nicknamed Eddie the Eagle, who flew like a wounded duck but never wanted for British pluck.]

Freestyle. Unlike ski jumping, freestyle has no dignity whatever. Most of its forms were invented in America by daredevils who were inhaling some illegal substance before they put their skis on backwards.

Almost any sequence of gyrations on skis may be called freestyle if the contestant remains conscious enough to respond to questioning. The styles are borrowed from ballet, acrobatics, gymnastics, figure skating and a Sicilian fire drill.

The common factor is to have *fun*. If having fun is a strange concept to you—possibly because of a personal relationship that turned to slush—don't be discouraged. Whereas the slalom and the downhill and the ski jump are often referred to as "disciplines," there is a minimum of self-control in the freestyle. You just let your body express itself as it wants, on skis, and if someone says, "Wow, how did you do that?" you know that you have created a freestyle.

As a form of self-expression, freestyle depends a lot on your having a self to express. If after introspection you find that you are essentially selfless, you may be better suited to joining a monastic order that skis mainly to service the little brandy kegs borne by St. Bernards to rescue the stormbound.

Is it okay to express someone *else's* self in the freestyle? Certainly. Most freestylers do just that. They see someone on TSN performing a demented routine on skis, and they say, "Hey, I can do that." Words that make a fitting epitaph.

An indication of the degree of license to

The Takeoff

invent in the freestyle is found in the event's original name: *Hot Dog Skiing.* Translated to "Le Ski du Chien Chaud," this name perplexed Europeans. Aside from being required to cut the mustard, the hot-dogger had no relevance to a wiener clad in a bun doing somersaults. It was necessary to explain to them that *hot-dogging* means putting on an egregious display to celebrate an athletic feat. Because of this pejorative connotation, the correct generic term is now *freestyle skiing.*

Ballet. Forget the tutu. It's been done. And the ballerina suffered a frostbitten adagio. Just wear comfortable clothing that can be removed quickly in the event that your skiing interpretation of "The Dying Swan" requires an SPCA emergency team.

Since much of freestyle ballet is done backwards (sometimes on purpose), you need shorter skis than those for the downhill. Speed is not the primary object. No one cared how fast Anna Pavlova could run across the stage, and you too will be judged on points such as "elevation" (8,000 feet) and "attitude" (positive). Your shorter skis should enable you to perform ballet *pas* to express sorrow . . . elation . . . sensual excitement (wear tighter briefs).

Another help is the music. Ballet skiing is the only competitive form that involves musical accompaniment conveyed by loudspeakers. More expense, but your playing the mouth organ as you do your routine—even though the harmonica is wired to your mouth to free your hands to grip the ski poles—unduly complicates an already demanding art form.

On the plus side, you get to choose the music for your ballet. Tchaikowski's *Nutcracker* is a natural choice, though your dance of the sugarplum fairies could be short a few plums. A snippet of contemporary rock music should be more practical if you can find a group that isn't voicing a craving for death.

The national anthem? No. The less you are required to remain upright, the better.

The other good thing about ballet skiing is that you do your own choreography without affecting your sexual orientation so long as you take a few coffee breaks. You can ignore Balanchine, Diaghileff and the entire Russian school except perhaps Pavel Bure. Pavel has some neat moves that you may want to incorporate into your routine, and he earns bigger bucks than the Bolshoi.

The basic movements of ballet skiing are crossovers, kick turns, spins, tip rolls, jump turns and the even more basic bowel movement. Variations on these gyrations are the somersault and the handstand, which should never be performed in front of children or

Freestyle is all about personal expression.

people who are already confused about which side is up.

Many of these ballet moves are done on one ski, letting the other ski do pretty much as it likes. The critical requirement is, whatever happens, maintain an aesthetic look on your face as though your soul totally approves of your body acting like a windmill with the heaves.

Mogul Skiing. Perfect for the competitive skier who has no ambition to look graceful. In fact it was only in 1992 that mogul skiing was accepted as a Winter Olympics event because poorer countries couldn't afford the extra medical insurance.

What *is* a mogul? A mogul is a hump, bump or lump varying in size from a small bulge in the terrain to Mount Matterhorn. Contrary to popular belief, moguls are not formed by letting fallen snow settle on the bodies of downhillers who made a serious error in judgment. The truth is that mogul-making is deliberate defacement of a perfectly good slope. Skiers are allowed to carve out these cruel ridges and ruts, often howling at the full moon, before returning to their daytime jobs as divorce lawyers and aluminum siding salesmen.

The mogul competition consists of winning judges' points for speed (25 percent), jumps (25 percent), turns (50 percent) and occult acts of levitation (no points, but polite applause). Falling down does not disqualify you so long as your recovery is not unduly prolonged by a search for your head.

Because mogul skiing is more physically demanding than rational styles, it is not recommended for people over sixty-five. The amount of jumping, in particular, tests the legs, which may be as much as six inches shorter at the end of the run. On the other hand, moguls may well suit very tall women who seek a wider choice of dance partners. A few seasons of mogul racing and you can feel comfortable dating Mickey Rooney.

[Cautionary note: do not wear breakaway pants when doing moguls. Stunts such as the "daffy" position (jumping while doing the splits in midair and making a funny face) can rupture your jeans at the crotch, causing sudden exposure to frigid air and possible loss of something more important than judges' points.]

Aerials. Freestyle aerial jumping is for skiers who are really scared of growing old. It is the only competitive skiing event regularly sponsored by the makers of neck braces. Before you attempt aerials, you should ask yourself: "Am I wheelchair accessible? Do I covet a career mouth-painting Christmas cards? Wouldn't it be more sensible to satisfy my exhibitionism by buying an old raincoat and flashing where it's safer?"

However, if reason is no object, you should at least understand that aerial jumps such as the double-back somersault need rehearsal. Preferably in the presence of a brigade of St. John's Ambulance. Freestyle aerialists have learned, with the help of casualty figures, to train by using a trampoline to vault into a swimming pool instead of ice. *The pool must be filled with water.* A waterless swimming pool is, if anything, even less forgiving than snow to land in.

Now you ask: "Does this mean I have to learn how to swim?"

Answer: not really. Being able to swim while wearing six-foot-long skis is a very special skill, more of an aquatic sport than alpine. The practical solution is to bounce off the trampoline *without* wearing your skis, performing the somersault, spread-eagle, backscratcher, daffy, helicopter, etc., before landing in the pool barefoot. If you still drown, the whole business may attract the attention of the coroner. This is why you should *never* perform freestyle aerials without being accompanied by someone who can explain to the authorities what happened.

CHAPTER 9

Terrestrial Skiing

Return to Planet Earth

CROSS-COUNTRY is safer than cross-city skiing because there is less chance of straddling a fire hydrant. Also, cross-city skiing is pretty much restricted to the brief period between a heavy fall of snow and the arrival of snowplowing vehicles, some coming sideways with the horn blaring a challenge to your right to ski down the middle of the high street.

Cross-country, in contrast, can actually be relaxing. In relation to the downhill, you are less dependent on the law of gravity to get you into trouble, except when you are caught in an avalanche (see Chapter 11). Cross-country can also be a more sociable kind of skiing. Because it is usually done in single file, whole families can spend the day cross-country skiing without a word being spoken—a major source of domestic stability in Switzerland.

For the novice, cross-country is the ideal way to master the skating movement in private, away from prying eyes and coarse laughter. You can be totally alone on the ski trail. This raises the familiar philosophical question: If a skier falls in the forest, and no one hears him, how do we know that he made any sound before he froze to death? To avoid having to answer this conundrum, Scandinavians are likely to cross-country ski in groups of twenty or more, all following silently along the same two ruts in the snow for days and even weeks at a time. This would drive other peoples—Spaniards and like hot-blooded folk—completely mad. But you can't argue with one of the highest standards of living in the world.

An extension of this gregarious cross-country is the marathon, another Nordic specialty, in which thousands of skiers fan out across a snowy plain and keep poling along for distances up to ninety-five miles, or spring thaw, whichever comes first.

These marathon races are noted for their informality, beginners and experts mingling and keeping warm with beverages other than Gatorade, served at regular intervals. To enjoy the cross-country marathon, all you really have to do is wear a bib with a large number on it and push fluids.

Less convivial is the activity of the solitary cross-country skier who glides along the marked trail, absorbing the spiritual tonic of a winter wonderland, with no technical problems other than how to pee against a tree. Some trail skiers find that just the sight of a melting icicle drizzling water stimulates the bladder. Being miles from the nearest restroom can therefore create a minor crisis not readily relieved. Very few ski resorts bother to post the international silhouette figures for the Men's tree and the Women's tree. This almost justifies your marking your trail with yellow dimples in the snow as some insurance against getting lost. But this may disgust other skiers who are trying to escape just such reminders of their mortality.

In this regard, you are less likely to offend if you stick to *off-trail* cross-country, going where no man has gone before, and few women. Or if they did, they haven't tinkled there since the last snowfall. Nor has the trail been groomed into parallel tramlines that can bring on delusions of a San Francisco trolley car and crazed cries—"Ding! Ding!"—that disturb the peace.

Instead, you choose your own route. And having made your selection of trackless waste, you may notice a sign that says: DANGER! NO SKIING BEYOND THIS POINT. How should you respond to this warning? If you are under twenty-one years of age, you will of course ignore it. Defying authority is, for you, part of the thrill of cross-country. Even if you ski only a couple of yards beyond the sign and beat your chest with your fists, you have given the old testosterone a workout. Older cross-country buffs, too, may see the sign as the work of mischievous trolls trying to lure humans away from their Festival of the Ice Maiden. But you, as a mature adult, will do well to hesitate before giving the sign the nasal fingerwave and plunging willy-nilly into the forest (see Chapter 11, "Survival Gear").

For those who insist on being competitive, cross-country ski racing affords what is probably the least exciting spectator sport in the world, not excepting nursing-home croquet. The contestants lugubriously pole themselves along two ruts in the snow for fifteen miles or more, eyes fixed firmly on the unrelenting course, in a test of endurance that prepares them for a life as chartered accountants, married, with five children.

Cross-country ski tracks often lead to derailments.

If the racer behind is so inconsiderate as to overtake, you are required to move off the track, into a snowdrift, and wait till she or he has passed you. Sticking out a pole to trip the interloper is against the rules and therefore should not be attempted unless you are well out of sight of the judges posted along the trail. To try to tart up this event, its devotees have introduced the cross-country relay. Instead of passing a baton, the racer touches her teammate, who accelerates briskly after being spiked with a ski pole.

Another cross-country showstopper is the biathlon. Contrary to popular belief, biathletes are not skiers who swing both ways. Certainly not while carrying a rifle. Actually, the biathlon is a timing event comprising skiing a circular course and pausing four times to shoot at targets, twice standing, twice prone, but always blinded by driving snow. For obvious reasons, the biathlon is not much of a spectator sport either. It attracts people who would like to be Renfrew of the Mounted without having to take care of a horse. Canadians of both genders do quite well in international biathlon competition, though there is little chance that the rifle will replace the hockey stick as the nation's deadly weapon of choice.

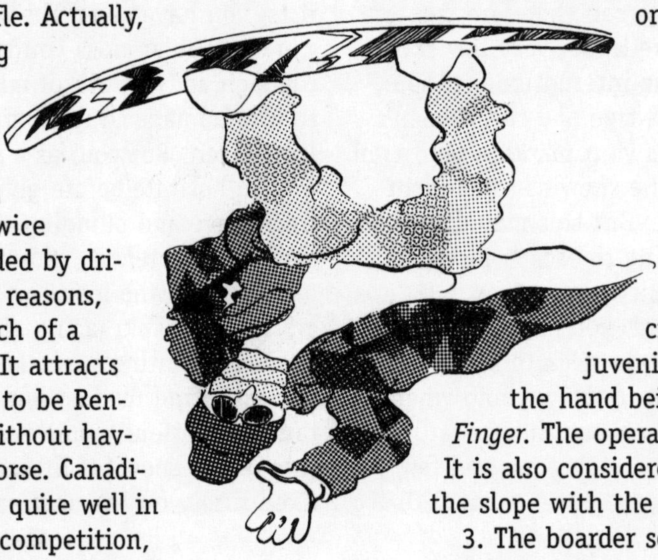

Snowboarding. "Grays on trays." That is the derogatory term used by youthful snowboarders to describe the adults who are starting to take up this frenetic pastime.

"Brats on slats" is the retort of the older practitioners, glaring out of their foxholes.

Such is the generation gap which, for the time being, has supplemented the other gullies, drop-offs, pipes and traditional slit-trenches that are the favorite terrain of these kamikaze kids. Or, in their own parlance, "rippers."

Snowboarding is, of course, the mongrel whelp of surfing, probably born when the wheels fell off some hyper teen's skateboard. It differs from conventional skiing in several ways, aside from being certifiable:

1. Snowboarding uses one plank instead of two. This does not mean that, having lost one ski to a ravine, you can use the remaining one to snowboard. The board is shorter and wider than a ski, and is usually painted with a garish, psychedelic design to ward off evil spirits, such as parents. The bottom of the board—exposed during flying leaps and turns—is often personalized with the owner's message (READ THIS AND DIE), or simply the classic skull and crossbones.

2. No poles. The boarder must find something else to do with his hands besides supporting his scarecrow sleeves. For the juvenile this is not a problem, the hand being the agent of *The Finger.* The operative digit in boarding. It is also considered cool to swoop down the slope with the hands in the pockets.

3. The boarder sets his feet sideways, rather than facing forward, because his seeing where he is going is irrelevant.

Snowboard equipment is less costly than that for polite skiing, but not much. It is a mistake to think that you can get by with using your mother's old ironing board—especially if your mother is hanging on to it. A serviceable board will cost several hundred dollars. It must be made of spacecraft material because if it sunders at high speed, you can suffer a severe case of bifurcation more painful than a split personality.

Ideally, and to look cool to the point of icing up, you will buy a 157-centimeter Mike Estes signature-model board, personally autographed by the manufacturer and accompanied by an affidavit swearing that this model has been sold to no one over twenty-three years of age. (You may need your birth certificate.)

As for outerwear, this is becoming more regimented than during the primitive days of boarding (last week). In that time the prescribed garb was super-baggy pants and equally sloppy joe sweater. This raiment helped to distinguish the boarder from the skier, who wore form-fitting stuff and was therefore *elderly*. But with the advent of the professional snowboarder, needing a svelte background for his sponsor's decals, the okay threads are more sharply defined:

1. Tailored nylon jacket and pants, retro-colored to match old automobiles like the Mustang. ($250 each)

2. Boarding boots. Formerly ex-army boots, like the ones other kids said your mother wears. ($275)

3. Boarding gloves. Must be supple enough to permit tying bootlaces in midair. Removable linings for washing to promote hygiene for kids who formerly considered washing anything to be a form of sacrilege. Retro-shade, nylon-shelled. ($125)

4. Boarding goggles. Retro-framed to resemble those of World War I fighter pilots. (White silk scarf optional.) Goggles equipped with defroster and tiny windshield wipers may have to be ordered direct from Germany. ($40+)

5. Boarding toque, or tuque, as in being tuque to the cleaners. ($29.99)

6. Board bag, in which to carry the board, the boots and the welfare cheque. So neat is the board bag that you may be able to skip all the other cool stuff and just swagger around with the bag slung over your shoulder. ($99.95)

7. Après-boarding sweats. Must be *very* cool to absorb the perspiration. Either go for 100 percent cotton or lounge in front of the resort's fireplace smelling like a wet goat. ($69)

8. Boardinghouse. May be cheaper than buying or renting accommodation.

Although the equipment required for snowboarding is showing signs of conformism, the sport itself remains anarchic. The boarder's movements are unpredictable, second only to those of people tobogganing on an old inner tube. This continues to lead to tension between conventional skiers and boarders who fancy that they can coexist on the same slope. Some of the language exchanged is said to contribute to early thaw of the snowpack, if not global warming. While there are few recorded cases of the conflict escalating to serious physical violence, there may be bodies buried in alpine meadows where the wildflowers have never bloomed in such riotous profusion.

Recently, special slopes have been allotted to snowboarders, but the numbers of boarders are increasing faster than the hoped-for attrition by fatal injuries.

Continuing conflict between skiers and boarders over *lebensraum* seems inevitable. God *is* making more mountains, but the process takes millions of years, too long for people already exasperated by waiting in line for the ski lift.

It will be a pity if the UN has to send in peacekeepers to create a buffer zone between warring skiers and boarders. Having to pass through Blue Beret checkpoints every hundred yards or so down the slope will put a damper on the youthful excesses that are a vital part of alpine sport.

To help avoid the ugly snowball fight that escalates into World War III, observe a few pacifying rules:

1. If you bowl over a skier, don't stop to cut another notch in your board, then zoom on. You might seriously consider helping the flattened oldster to his or her feet, with some noncommittal remark such as "I admit no legal liability for your colliding with my snowboard."

2. Don't address a skier as "Polecat!" Hilarious though the sally is, you may discover that a ski pole can smart when inserted up a sensitive orifice.

3. Recognize that the little people you enjoy terrorizing are not necessarily aged midgets. Some are young children. Who will not understand your yelling, "Go back to the rest home!"

The strongest civilizing influence on snowboarders is the sport's admission to the Winter Olympics. You may feel threatened by respectability. The Olympics being a commercialized industry, you face the loss of the in-your-face renegade spirit, even relegation to the phantasm of the other Abominable Snowman. Prepare to grieve.

Helicopter Skiing. For heli-skiing it helps if you own your own chopper. No, not the kitchen knife. The airplane. A bit pricey for most people. Rent-a-Wreck? Not recommended. A previously owned whirlybird may not have many miles on the odometer, but that's because it mostly goes up and down. You don't want to entrust your life to some radio station's former bleary eye-in-the-sky. Or, indeed, any aircraft that is afraid of heights.

The usual way to heli-ski is to look around Canada's Rocky Mountains till you find a place where someone owning a helicopter uses it to take groups of daredevil skiers to mountaintops and drop them in the snow. WARNING: they charge for this service. Several dollars. In fact, heli-skiing is pretty well limited to rich people (i.e., those owning their own country), who have learned that they have a terminal disease and want to go out in style.

Reason for the expense: the helicopter comes with a pilot who does this sort of thing for a living since his wife left him for another woman. The fare, plus tip, may shock you unless you are sharing the cost with a group of more people than the aircraft is authorized to carry. Crowded into a small chopper, with everyone's skis, you may experience claustrophobia as well as vertigo during the flight. Antianxiety medication could be indicated, but you should keep in mind that pills like Gravol can have a sedative effect, and you don't want to doze off while shussing down Mount Robson.

In Europe, heli-skiing is banned by most countries to protect the environment. They have found that the downdraft and landings of choppers on their Alps cause avalanches that can wipe out an entire village, creating hostility in the people buried alive. No such restriction exists in Canada, where the alpine villages are less picturesque and therefore expendable.

For this reason Canadian heli-skiing attracts many wealthy Europeans and Japanese, and in the event that your helicopter is unable to recover from landing upside down, you could find yourself stamping a message in the snow that requires an interpreter in potential air rescue craft.

However, these hazards are said to be fully worth risking, given the incomparable thrill of skiing down an immaculate slope of deep, powder snow. The experience has been described as a spiritual orgasm. Which is repeated time after time, as long as the heli-pilot can get it up. It is the only orgy approved by Tourism Canada.

Heli-skiing—Be sure to board the right helicopter.

CHAPTER 10

Ski Conditions

The Good, the Bad, the Pits

SNOW. How important to skiing is snow? This depends on whether you go outside the ski lodge. Some skiers develop an unhealthy dependency on snow and can't enjoy a skiing holiday without it. We should remember that *snow* is a street name for cocaine. Which is also addictive. True, we rarely see a skier snorting nonnarcotic snow—on purpose, that is—but there have been cases of skiers on withdrawal trying to lick the frost off their freezer.

Anyway, *legalized* snow is pretty well confined to winter months, flourishing best when the weather is cold. Some skiers believe that God created snow just to prevent having most of humankind bunched up around the Equator.

To identify the winter months, you need to know which hemisphere you are in. The Northern or the Southern. You can always ask a police officer, but often your parents, though otherwise uninformative, will be able to tell you whether your skiing months are December–April or April–December. Another clue is if you see crocodiles on the slope.

If we assume that you live in the Northern Hemisphere, you may start moving towards the mountains as early as November. This is the month when the first snow appears on the peaks, the sight of which causes certain hormonal changes in the skier, a rush normally associated with foreplay or stag films. The eye pupils dilate, breathing becomes heavier and saliva may dribble from the corners of the mouth. In cities like Vancouver, British Columbia, where office buildings often afford a clear view of the snow-mantled North Shore mountains, the work ethic goes into remission. In some

Ski Conditions: the Good.

employees it is cured permanently (see Chapter 12 "Ski Bums").

As the winter months pass, the snow on the mountains gets deeper and more accessible to skiers who are afraid of heights. By February, the snow should be down to sea level, so you can ski on flat places like airports, though this is not recommended.

The Inuit are said to have more than forty words for snow in its various forms, and those are just the printable ones. A glossary of snow's different meanings will be found at the end of this book over the authors' dead bodies.

The North American Indians have a saying: "Little snow, big snow; big snow, little snow." This cryptic adage baffled the early white pioneers, causing many to head south. The only snow they understood was the one-size-fits-all kind. But all that the Indians meant, of course, was that "little snow"—i.e., small flakes—is the sort that results in much snow, while "big snow"—descending doilies—mostly melts on hitting the ground. The skier therefore prays for little snow because there will be lots.

All skiers seek the *perfect* snow. This can become a holy quest, almost fanatical in its intensity. The pilgrim falls to his knees—always dodgy on skis—when he or she at last has a vision of the Virgin Slope.

The *ne plus ultra* of snows is *powder.* Powder is fluffy new snow. God's way of covering the wrinkles on the face of Mother Earth: Powder. *Light powder* is ideal for skiing, when supported by older, more compacted snow—the family situation without the nagging about finding a job.

Melting snow is snow that has been abused by a higher temperature. Normally, we would not think of the sun as a bad influence, but the fact is that solar rays are responsible not only for freckles but for the curse of melting snow. Try not to be bitter. Our sun does serve some useful purposes—photosynthesis, lighting the moon, etc.—so cursing and throwing lumpy slush at the star is indiscreet though understandable.

A particularly sneaky kind of melting snow is found on the eastern slopes of the Rockies, which are subject to a sudden, dry wind called a *Chinook.* Terrible tales are told of skiers caught in a mountain Chinook, of the snow melting faster than they can ski down the hill till, abruptly, they are overtaken by thaw, engulfed by spring wheat and devoured by hungry gophers.

Another formidable foe of skier's snow is the Pineapple Express, the Pacific warm front that often sweeps up from Hawaii to create monsoon conditions in the coastal mountains. This interminable warm downpour turns the early snow into what the Indians call *mashed potato.* Ski-resort owners prefer to describe the slop as "humidity-challenged powder," but still have difficulty preventing the onset of depression among guests pay-

Ski Conditions: the Bad.

ing $200 a night to stand in a puddle. Instead of receiving tips, hotel employees have bite marks to show for their services.

To try to create instant powder, ski facilities bring out their snowblowers. These machines produce snow as a kind of refrigerated vomit. Or utility-grade blizzard. It lacks the quality of mercy, which droppeth like the gentle snow from Heaven, but is better than having to give guests their money back.

When mushy snow freezes because of a cold snap, it forms a crust known as *ice.* Skiing on ice can be interesting because there is no way of stopping other than by running into an object larger than yourself. So, do your ice-skiing *below* the tree line. Otherwise you may keep hurtling downward and up again into the next range of mountains. This is also known as *glacier skiing,* a very specialized category of the sport in that the slope moves instead of the skier (if he has any sense). Glaciers often break off, or calve, into the ocean, which is no way for you to switch to water skiing.

Ski Lifts. "How do I get up the mountain in the first place?" This is a common question asked by the novice skier who is stalling for time. He has bought his skis, boots and accident insurance, has driven to the ski resort, put on his gear, and now stands waiting for an elevator to take him up—which he senses to be the proper direction in order to come down.

Ah-ha! No elevator. At least nothing like the lift in his apartment building. Ski lifts are quite unique methods of ascent, requiring skills comparable to those of astronauts but without the countdown to launch.

The ski lift may be thought of as an aerial tumbril. Often the passengers have the same facial expression and body language as the French nobles headed for their appointment with Madame in La Place de la Concorde. They know that they are being herded to a new experience in their lives, but are not sure that it is a far, far better thing they do than they have ever done.

While ski lifts are generally less hazardous than hiking up a snow-covered mountain without radar, certain activities are not compatible with this mode of levitation:

1. Sexual intercourse with more than two persons (simultaneously). Limited space dictates a degree of moderation, even if it means making two trips.

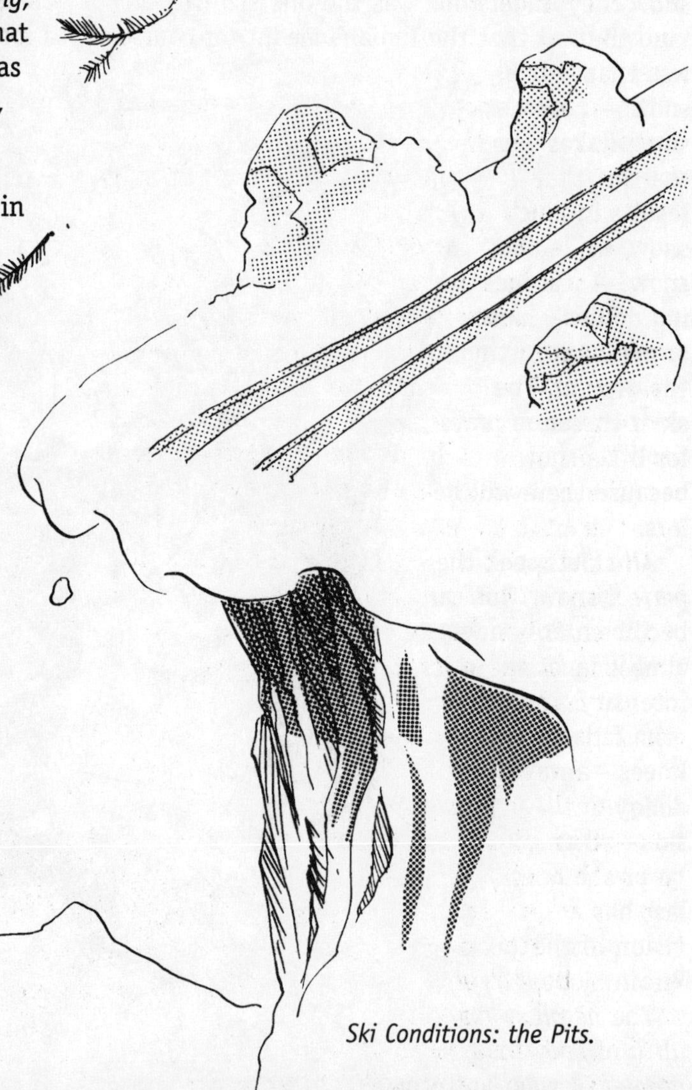

Ski Conditions: the Pits.

2. Forgetting that you are not on a porch swing and falling asleep. (This can happen if you have drunk your après ski as an avant ski.)

3. Spitting on skiers below. Remember the old homily: "Be nice to people on the way up because you will meet them again on the way down."

The Gondola. As elegant as ascension can get without being capitalized. Does a gentleman remove his toque when a lady enters the gondola? Not if he is bald.

The gondola is a cable car that rises between steel pylons staggered up the mountainside and behooving a degree of trust in engineering that borders on the credulous. It is not unusual for the cable to get fouled in a pulley, halting the gondola several hundred feet above a rock face. To be swinging helplessly in the wind like this can be a test of your ability to carry on a casual conversation. And even downright embarrassing, since the gondola does not have a lavatory.

If you react anally to stress, it may be more prudent for you to wait till a large bird carries you up the mountain, even though this extends the ascent by a day or two.

[Note: even an incident-free ride in a crowded gondola will be a supreme test of your deodorant. Closely packed passengers, perspiring from pores long thought to be dormant, will steam up windows and warp the cheaper skis. Don't be the eye of the storm: before you enter the gondola soak yourself in an industrial-strength air freshener. Being tossed out of a moving cable car can be a bad start for your day on the hill.]

The Chair Lift. If you have ever taken a ride on a Ferris wheel, you know the basic principle of the chair lift. Except, instead of revolving in one place, the chair lift has fewer pauses for uncontrolled passion. It is an endless belt of benched persons savoring the last few moments before their skis come into contact with reality. A moment of prayer is in order, especially if you bought your skis at the flea market.

The good thing about the chair lift, compared with the gondola, is that it is closer to the ground in the event that you fall off. A much better chance of survival. In fact, the most perilous phase of the chair lift is the dismounting. Ejecting from a relentlessly moving chair onto the reception slope for the first time on skis, with skiers behind in equally dire straits, you can create a scene of jumbled chaos that recalls Tennyson's "Battle Charge of the Light Brigade" . . . "Into the mouth of Hell rode the Six Hundred." Mounted on skis. Pure carnage.

Departing the chair lift makes you know how garbage feels being discharged into a landfill. Don't let things pile up. Get out of the reception area as quickly as possible before Greenpeace arrives to condemn the burial of toxic waste.

[Note: because of the increasing popularity of the sport, all ski lifts are being speeded up, and two-seaters converted to four-, six- and even eight-seaters—something to keep in mind if you have a problem getting off the escalator at Eaton's.]

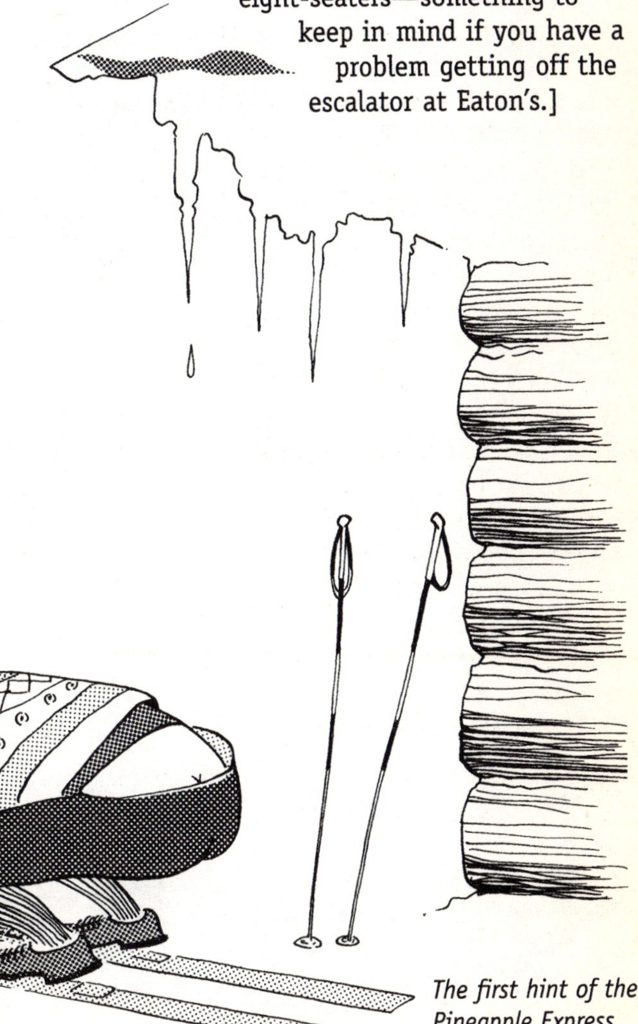

The first hint of the Pineapple Express.

Your gondola should look something like this . . .

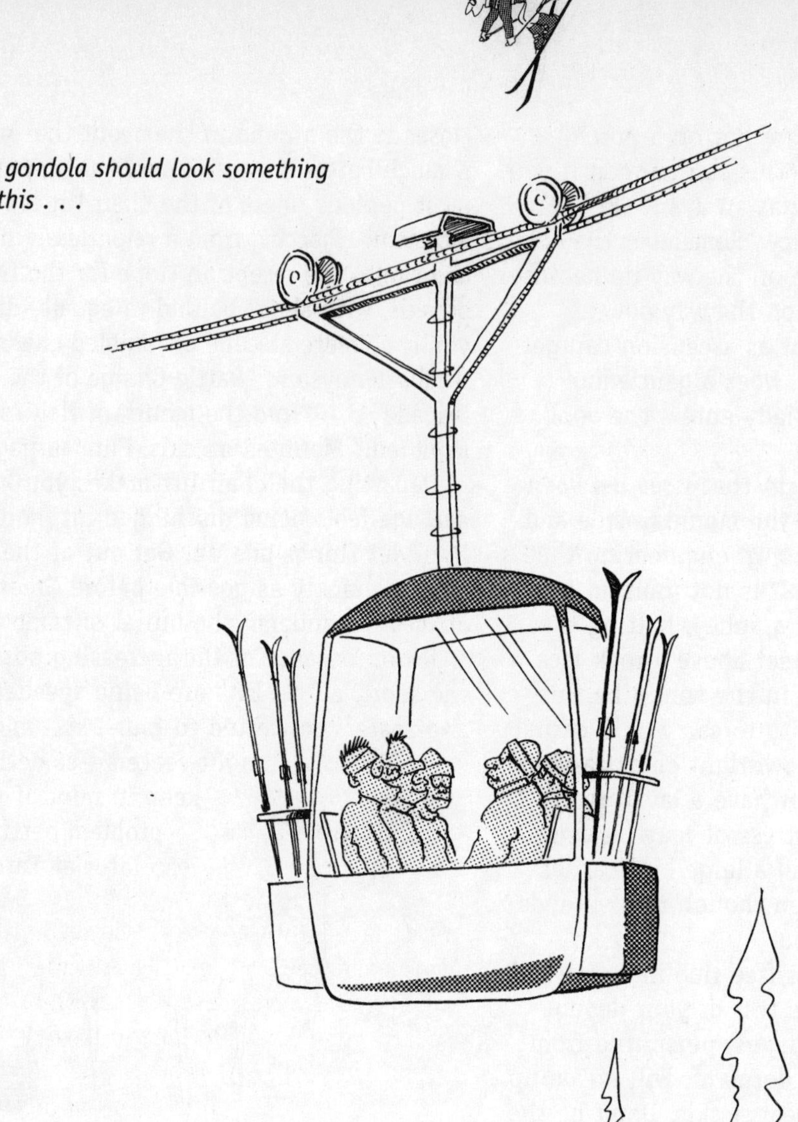

If the gondola you're on looks like this, you probably made a wrong turn at an Alp.

The Tow Lift. This is a chair lift whose bottom fell out. Easy to understand. If you have had any experience with straphanging in bus, tram or stagecoach, you will readily grasp the operating principle of the tow lift.

The Rope Tow is the most primitive type of tow lift. If you have to use the rope tow—a continuous length of twine with handholds at intervals—you know that you are on a low-budget hill and may want to wear a *Phantom of the Opera* mask.

Rope tows are powered by a hunchback named Igor. Let him pass before you try to grab the rope. You will need both hands to hold on to the rope, which means you carry your ski poles in your teeth. Also, it is important to notice when you have reached the top of the hill because that is where you should release the rope in the unlikely event that your hands are not frozen to it. Riding the rope tow back *down* the hill and possibly backwards is considered to be bad form, regardless of how you try to cover up by yodeling excerpts from *The Sound of Music.*

The T-Bar is more sophisticated than the rope tow. An inverted T (i.e., ⊥) the t-bar links to a continuous cable and catches you behind the thighs with the business end. *Do not* try to sit on the t-bar. Unless you have prehensile cheeks on your rear, you will promptly slide off the bar, your splayed skis presenting a picket fence to the t-bar riders behind you. Just rest *gingerly* against the bar, your tush at half-mast, so to speak, and let the cable empower your skis, and ultimately your whole body, onward and upward.

The main drawback of the t-bar: it is seating for two. Otherwise it is as unbalanced as you are for trying to ride it alone. You need to get to know another skier, rather quickly, to share your T.

The Double Chair Lift

You won't have time to be choosy, asking the person about his or her weight or coming on cute ("Would you care to join the T-party?"). Regardless of whether you hope to continue the relationship after you get to the top of the hill, don't let it divert you from dismounting. Which is tricky enough. You and your partner must decide which of you is going to get off first. This is no time for gallantry or an exercise in radical feminism. Without a synchronized departure from the lift, the last person to leave gets dumped, an accident so rich in symbolism that you may never go skiing again.

Or, if you do, you will opt for the Poma lift. Invented by a crazed genius named Jean Pomagalski, this lift is also called the Platter-pull, the Button lift and the Schlep lift. The Poma is designed for the schlep, or single person, who is alone, for reasons best known to himself, but who still has the ambition to get to the top of the hill. Instead of the T, the Poma takes the shape of an upside-down floor lamp without the shade. The stem is embraced by your legs with the base supporting yours. Mounting this moving device requires such exquisite timing that the Poma is sometimes seen as a method of birth control. It is certainly better suited to the female skier than to the male, who after riding it up the hill could find that he is singing boy soprano. The abrupt start and spastic ride will test the mettle of persons with no rodeo experience in bulldogging steers.

Some general tactics for ski lifts:

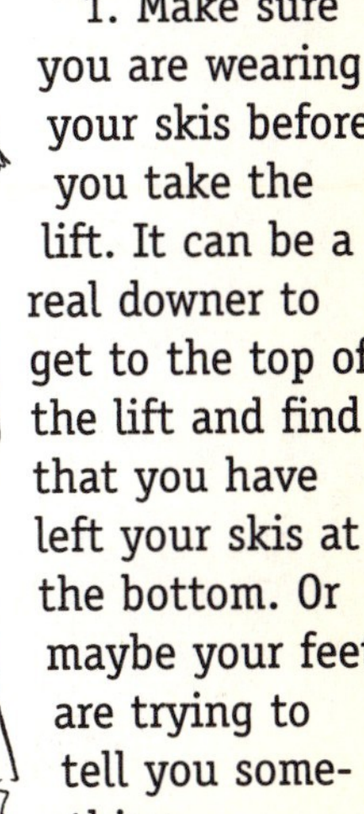

1. Make sure you are wearing your skis before you take the lift. It can be a real downer to get to the top of the lift and find that you have left your skis at the bottom. Or maybe your feet are trying to tell you something.

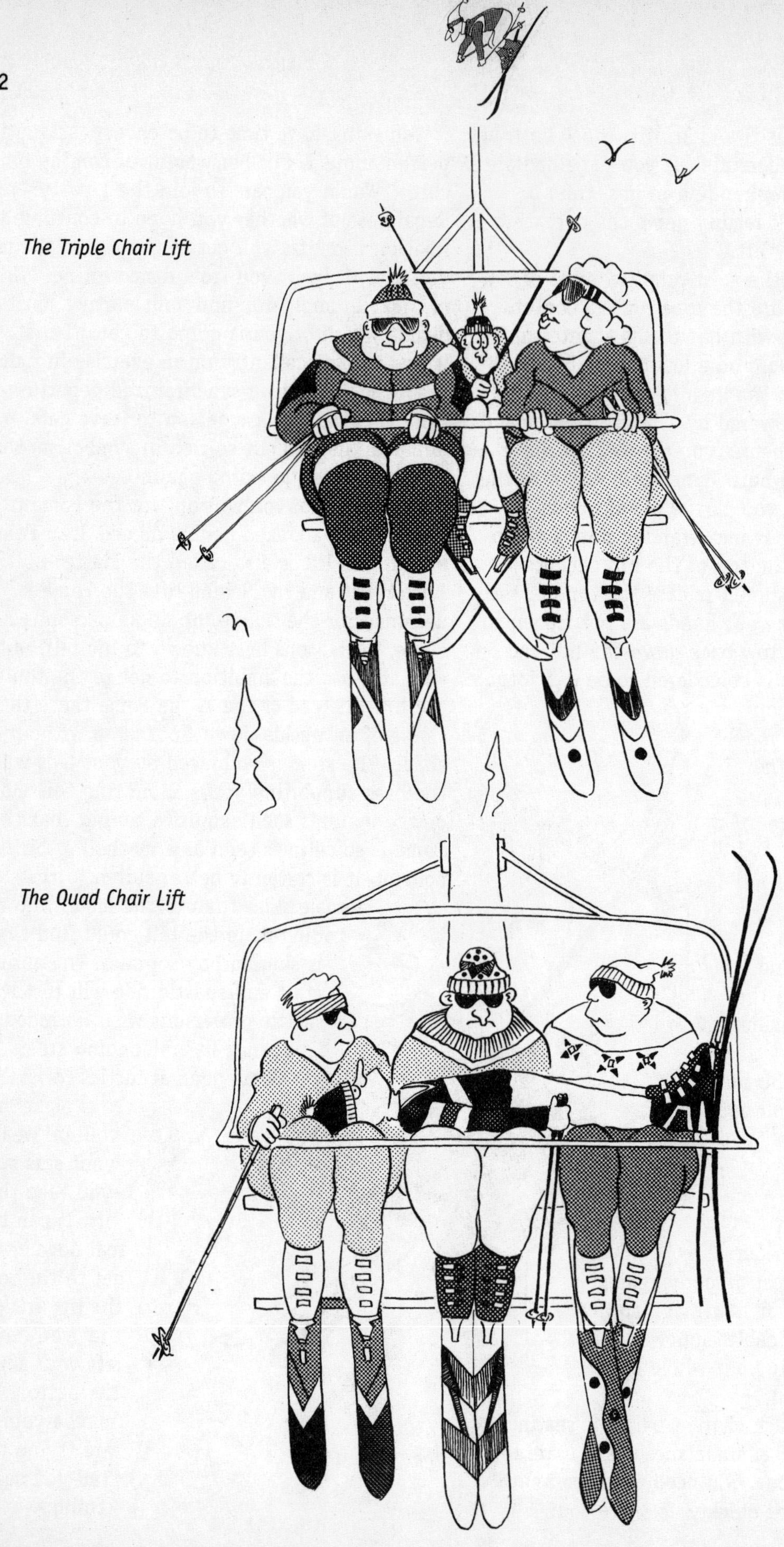

The Triple Chair Lift

The Quad Chair Lift

Ways to Ride a Rope Tow

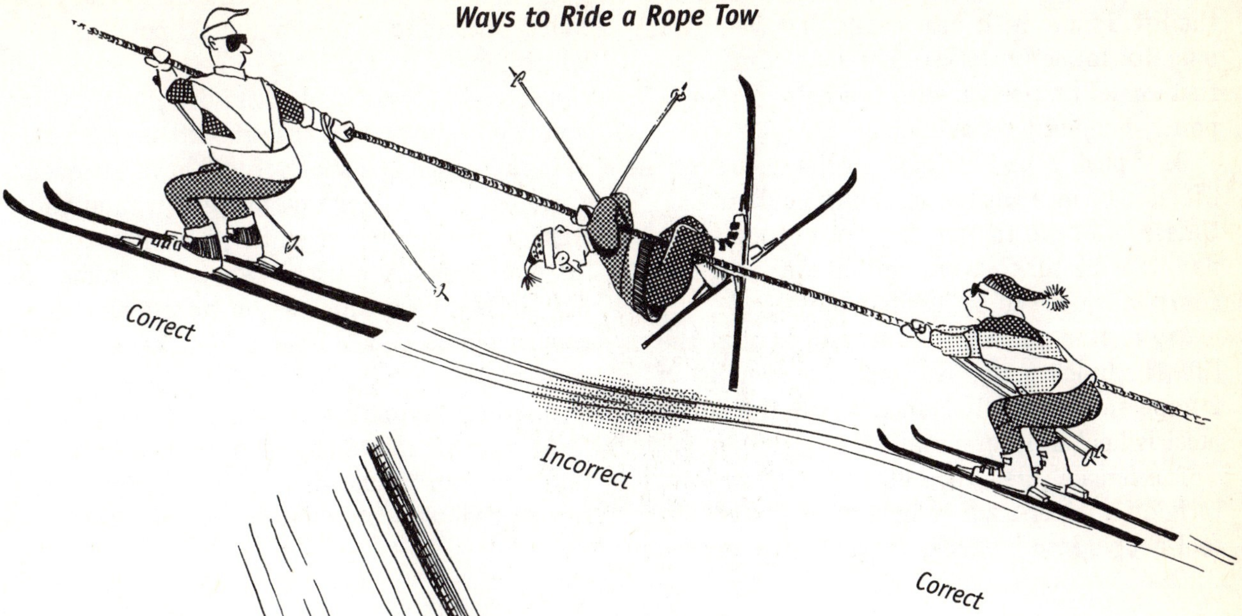

Correct

Incorrect

Correct

The Trouble with t-bars

2. You may be required to take a number for the lift. Ignore it. It just means that the lift operator formerly worked in a shoe store. It's first-come, first-serve, with the help of the pointy ends of your ski poles.

3. If push comes to shove in the queue for the lift, don't fence with other adults. Bully kids. Unless you have the fencing skills of a D'Artagnan, it is better to avoid perforations that the court will judge to be justifiable homicide.

Try to find out what is the rush hour at the lift. The lunch period is often recommended in Europe and especially France, where the noon meal is held in reverence.

The female skier who bulks up with clothing to feign a latter-stage pregnancy is not apt to fool people into breaking ranks. Pretty well every type of fake disability has been tried, and has failed, including camouflaging ski poles as a white cane.

[Note: whatever kind of ski lift you are using, you need a ticket. Because the lift is not free. This can come as a shock if you have assumed there would be no charge for seniors, and you went to the trouble of renting a walker. The only distinction made in lift tickets is that some are day tickets, others are season tickets and still others require you to open a joint bank account.]

Q: Where should I carry my lift ticket?

A: Your lift ticket should be firmly scotch-taped to your forehead. This leaves your hands free to deal with children in the queue.

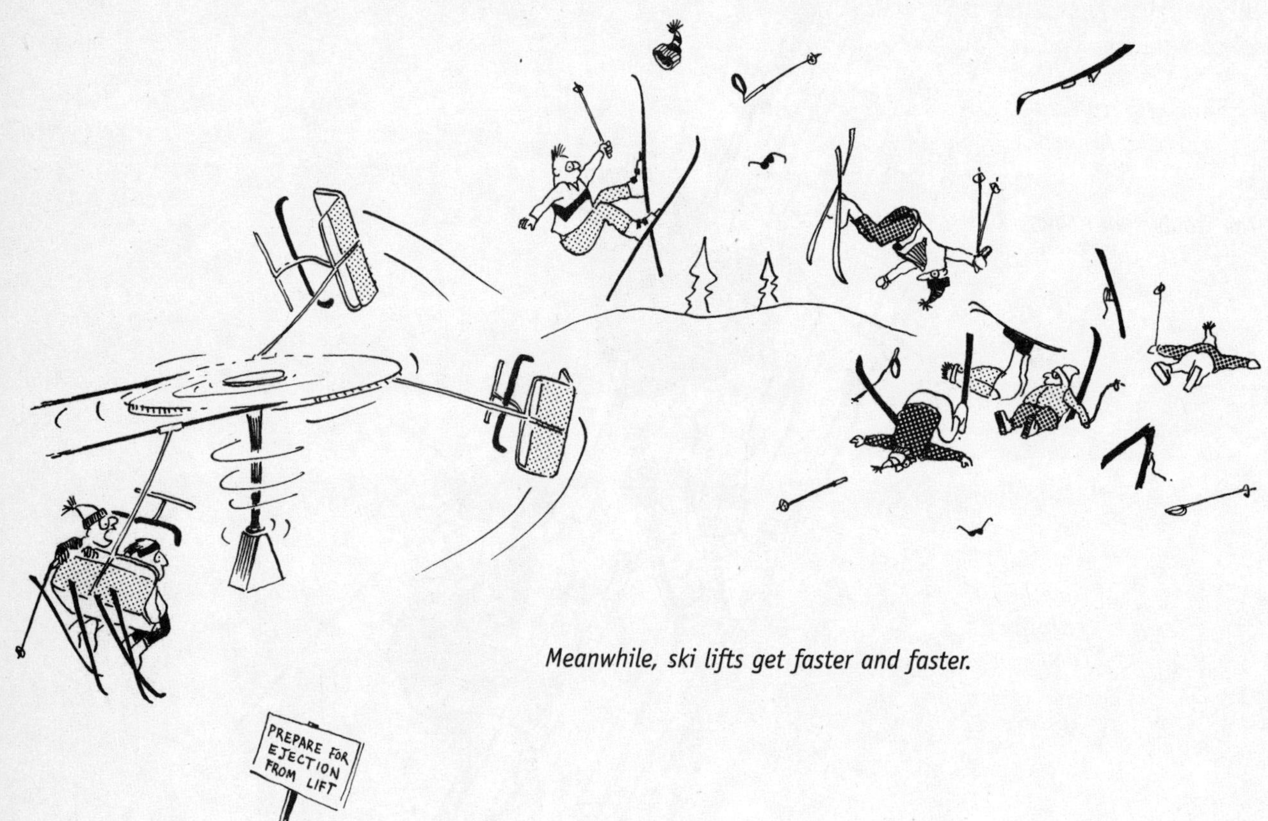

Meanwhile, ski lifts get faster and faster.

CHAPTER 11

Ski Survival

There's Cold in Them Thar Hills!

SNOW is like a top-flight fashion model: beautiful but cold. And because the skier's sport is so reliant on cold, his or her one surefire romance is that of flirting with *hypothermia.* Hypothermia is the condition of having abnormally *low* body temperature. It is sometimes confused with *hyperthermia,* which is having unusually *high* body temperature. If you are in doubt as to whether you have gone rigid because of hypo or hyper (but not Harpo), you can test your temperature with an instrument called a *thermometer.* However, your having to stand for one minute with a thermometer stuck in your mouth can result in your freezing to death, as well as looking like an extraterrestrial.

The best way for you, as a skier, to avoid hypothermia: *Wear clothes.*

Ski Survival Gear

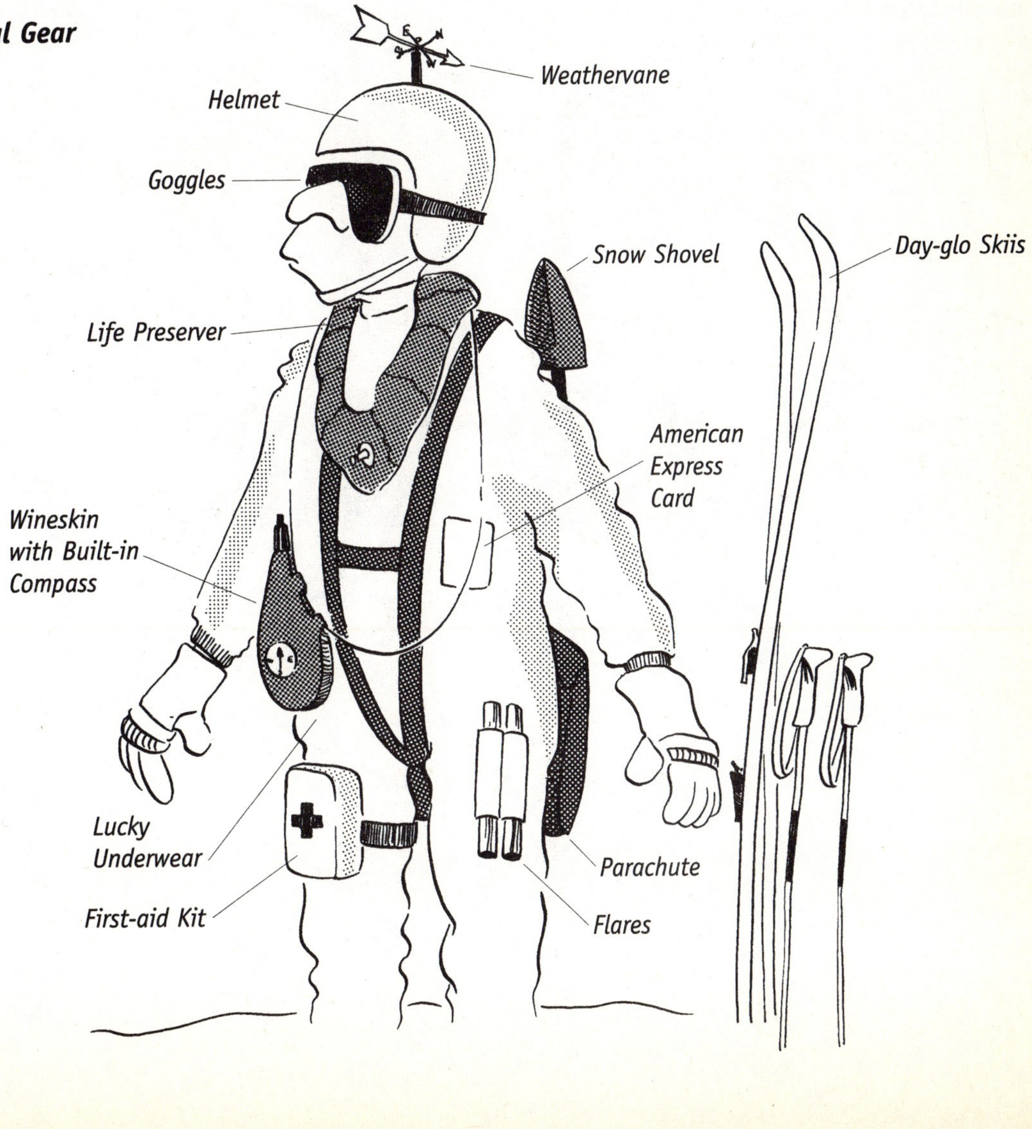

Don't be misled by TV shots of half-naked people sunning themselves in snowbanks. Those people are not skiing. They are trying to get a suntan without having to fly to Hawaii.

The *real* skiers are warmly dressed because they understand the importance of *insulation*. Think of your body as your home. This home has a certain amount of natural insulation, called *fat*. But your home does not have as much fat as a walrus, even though your overbite is competitive.

So, you need *extra* insulation to prevent your internal organs from hogging your blood supply. Imagine your blood supply to be the manager of a cheap hotel. The manager sees your nose, ears and other extremities as expendable. Doesn't care if you leave the ski slope with all your best features frozen off, looking like a takeout from *Tales From the Crypt*. That's cool with the blood supply. So long as your liver has remained warm and toasty, it's no sweat to the blood supply that someone is using your appendage to chill his Collins.

How do you tell when you are getting too cold to retain your members? *You start to shiver.* Shivering is how your body tries to generate heat without stretching the blood supply. But not all shivering is caused by your being cold. You may also be shivering as the result of sexual excitement. God only knows where your blood supply will end up then, and it may be better not to ask. If you are subject to ambiguous shivers, don't ski near persons you find attractive. Stay with the butt ugly. Then you will know that your shivering calls for putting more clothes *on*, rather than taking them off.

Spotting Hypothermia
Hint #1: Failure to get off the ski lift.

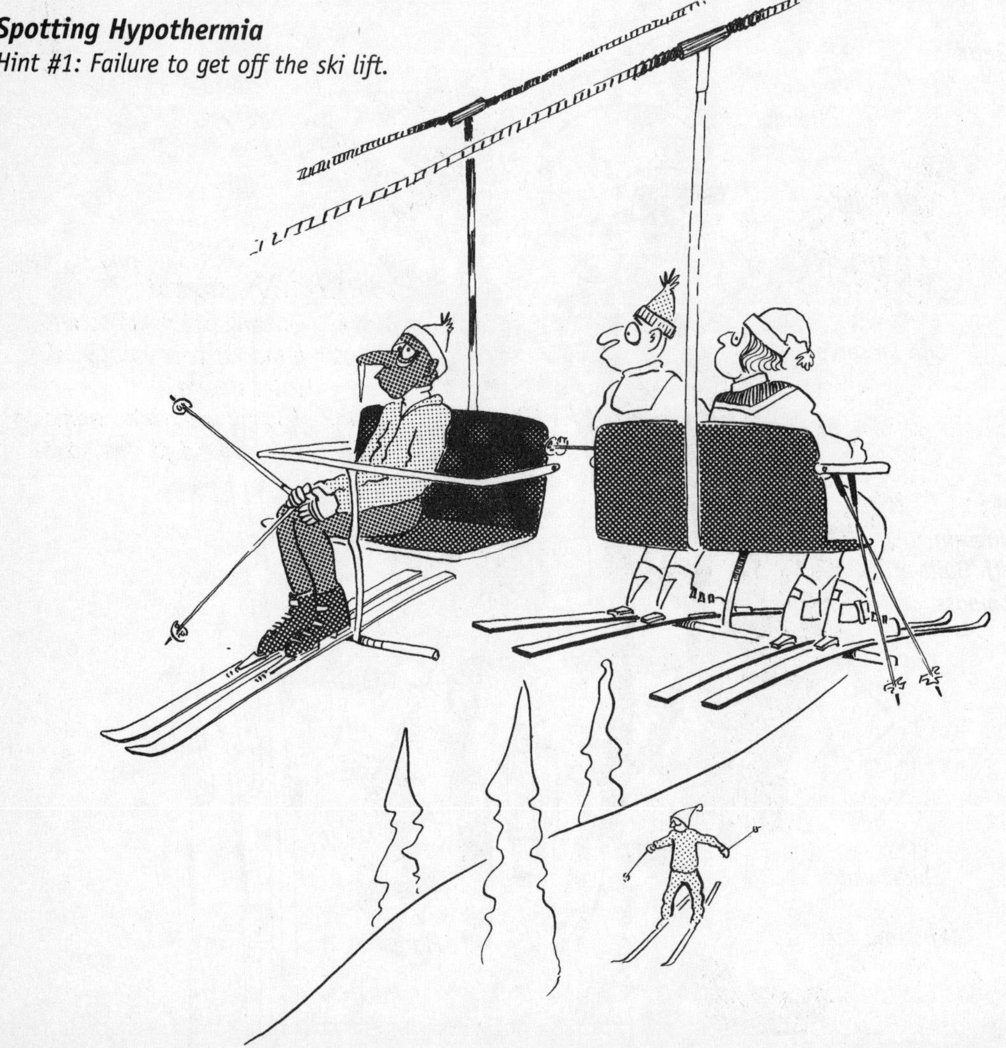

Spotting Hypothermia

Hint #2: Goggles iced-up.
Hint #3: Nose still on.
Hint#4: Skis still on (but has not moved in one hour).
Hint#5: Cigarette out.
Hint #6: No one home.

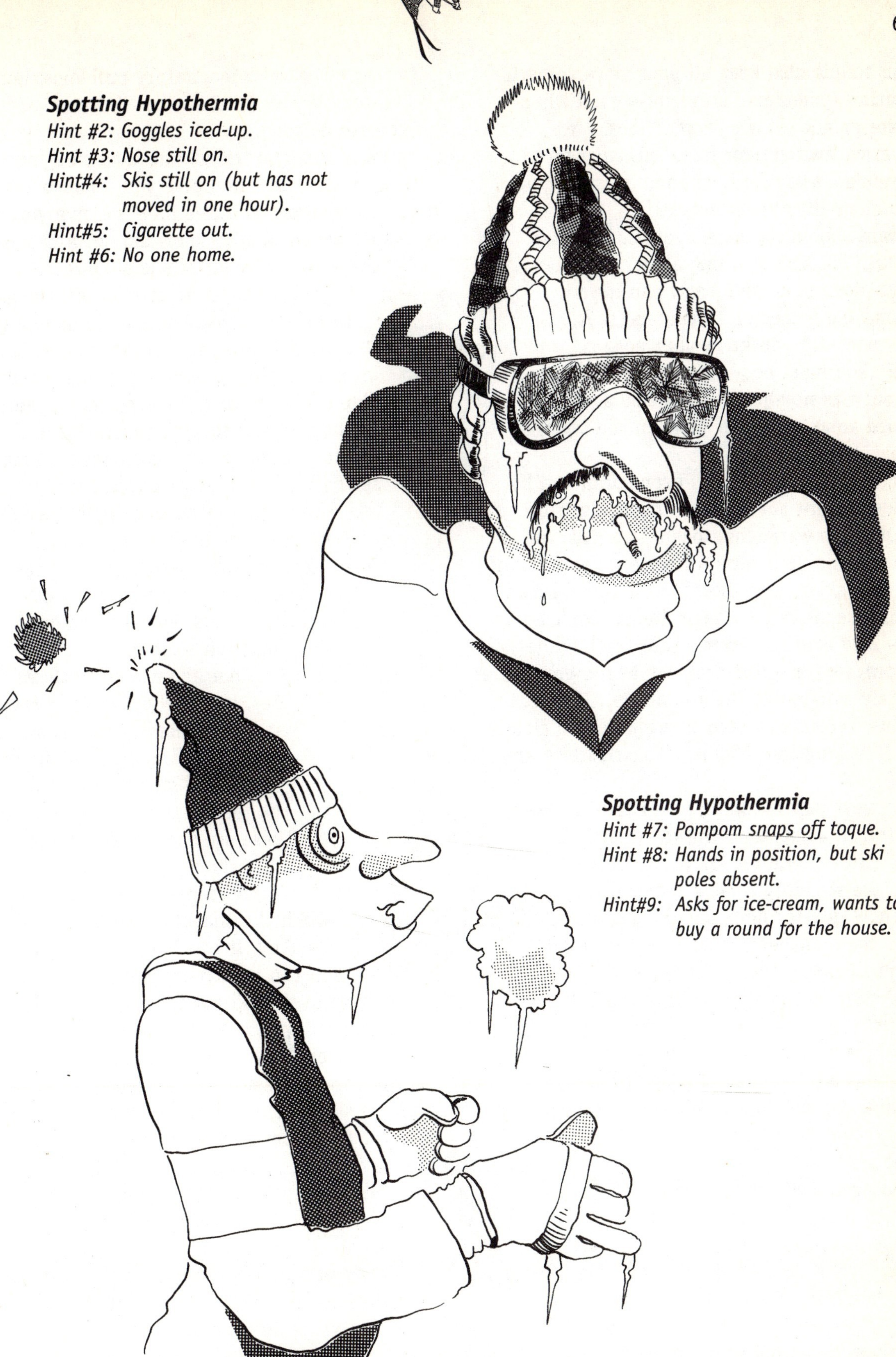

Spotting Hypothermia

Hint #7: Pompom snaps off toque.
Hint #8: Hands in position, but ski poles absent.
Hint#9: Asks for ice-cream, wants to buy a round for the house.

You should also keep all your movable parts in motion—simulated shivering—even when you are immobile. Wiggle your toes, wave your arms, twitch your face. This will move other skiers away from you and possibly give you a chair-lift seat to yourself.

Despite these measures, you may incur *frostbite.* The sneaky thing about frostbite is that often you don't know you have it till someone comes up to you and says, "Hey, man, did you know your nose is froze?" You must be alert to signs of frostbite, such as numbness, white spots on exposed areas and burst pipes in the crawl space.

When your frostbite has been confirmed by an independent survey, *don't panic.* Just use your hand to warm the frozen part. This can mean holding your nose for some time, possibly offending skiers who assume that you are commenting negatively on their aroma. Don't be drawn into conflict. Losing your teeth while saving your nose is a bad deal. Try to rub yourself as privately as possible (behind a tree). If this is not possible, accompany your massage with a clearly voiced explanation: "Goldarn this frostbite anyhow!"

The most painful phase of frostbite is when your frozen component thaws. It can take ten or fifteen minutes for you to defrost. If you are standing there screaming for the whole quarter hour, spooking other skiers, the management may feel obliged to put your head in their microwave.

Although losing a pinkie can smart, *altitude sickness* is serious. This potentially fatal ailment is caused mostly by *thin air.* Your lungs are likely accustomed to your breathing *fat* air. That is, air plumped up with oxygen. What your lungs are most comfortable with is sea-level air.

Below sea level, they have a problem with pressurization and Japanese trawlers. Above sea level, they can start laboring if you use an upper bunk. The fact is you lose 15 percent of your available energy for every 3,000 feet of altitude. So, before you do alpine skiing at 6,000 feet or more, you should be sure you have no history of heart or respiratory problems, indicated by your blacking out if seated in the theater balcony.

Does visiting a friend who lives in a high-rise apartment building give you a nosebleed? If so, skiing above the tree line can give you some spectacular nasal hemorrhaging. Although there may be some fringe benefit in bleeding to death in relative proximity to Heaven, consider that unlikely and carry a mile or so of toilet paper with which to plug your nostrils. This does oblige you to breathe through your mouth and possibly freeze your gums. Have the slope paged for a dentist. This is as good a time as any to have that root canal.

Should you wear an oxygen mask? If skiing at altitudes over 29,000 feet, yes. Let the Sherpas sneer if they choose. Their lungs are larger than yours, but how many of them have cable?

What about a snow shovel? Yes, definitely. The snow shovel is a *de rigueur* accessory when you are skiing outdoors in places like mountains, where the terrain tends to be uneven. These are the places susceptible to the skier's nightmare:

The Avalanche. An avalanche is when the snow has more fun than the skier. It can happen anywhere. You can be driving your car on the road to the ski facility and get buried under an avalanche. This solves your parking problem, but introduces the element of suffocating to death with a prepaid day-pass. Some skiing handbooks recommend that the would-be back-country skier attend an avalanche-training school. But it is almost impossible to train an avalanche, even if you have had some success with a poodle.

More practically you ought to take certain precautions to improve your relations with masses of rapidly moving snow:

1. Learn to recognize warning signs. ATTENTION! CLOSED! AVALANCHE DANGER

is not a veiled invitation to ski in that area. If you are skiing abroad, ACHTUNG GESCHLOSSEN-LAWINENGEFAHR! does not mean THIS WAY TO THE MEN'S ROOM!

2. Another warning sign is when the mountain above you suddenly goes *whoomf!* Mountains normally don't have much to say, so that when one of them goes *whoomf!* you can expect it to get a lot off its chest. And onto yours.

3. Don't believe that you can outrun an avalanche. Faith in your ski wax is misplaced, when you race against a wall of snow traveling at 100 mph, though it is a credit to your competitive spirit.

4. To reduce the chance of your being caught in an avalanche, some ski resort operators will advise you to ski only where avalanche-control gunners fire artillery shells into the slope to create a preemptive avalanche.

But before you ski blithely into the target area, consider whether the resort management has been given reason to hasten your room being made available to someone more civilized. Have you been sitting in front of the lounge fireplace in soggy Argyle socks? Drinking your martini through a straw? Wearing your skis in the dining room? In short, providing an excuse to direct you to a slope under bombardment? When the shells start bursting around you is no time to wish you had tipped the doorman.

Assuming that you *will* be caught in an avalanche, what survival gear should you have been buried with? Clearly, the snow shovel. Not your common household snow shovel, however. The skier's snow shovel is a much lighter model, made to be strapped to the bulging packsack that identifies you as a skier for whom speed is not everything, or indeed anything. The shovel may be used:

1. to dig your companion out of an avalanche.

2. to excavate a snow cave for yourself and your companion, or any number of guests who may drop in if the roof gives way.

3. to hibernate till spring. Either to have your cubs or simply to avoid Christmas shopping. If so, in addition to your snow shovel you will need to pack a sleeping bag, a flashlight and about 500 D-class batteries. (Whale oil *can* be used in lieu of electricity to light and heat your

igloo, but packing a whale is illegal unless you are a native person.)

Other items needed for your trek into the mountain wilderness:

A Compass. In case you get lost, this instrument will help you determine which direction is north. You can then ski south, confident that sooner or later you will hit Palm Springs, California.

A Whistle. To be used when lost. The main drawback—aside from attracting wild dogs—is that whistle echo, bouncing off mountains, can drive you crazy with false hopes of rescue.

An Inflatable Balloon. Another attention-getting device. To be seen by a search plane, your balloon will need to be big enough to advertise REMAX. Blowing it up could take a lot out of you.

Bread Crumbs. Leaving a trail of bread crumbs is particularly popular with the small birds that will eat them. Try not to get lost farther than fifty yards from a bakery. Or be prepared to carry more loaves than fit in your bread box.

An Avalanche Cord. The cord unwinds from a spool on the skier's waist, with a brightly colored plastic bottle on the end trailing behind you. The scientific principle involved here is that when you are trapped under an avalanche, the bottle will float to the surface, and when a rescuer tugs on the line, you can reel him in. Despite the good sales of the avalanche cord, there is no record of the cord's ever being instrumental in locating a buried skier. There are, however, many documented cases of the plastic bottle's getting snagged on a tree or another skier, causing the owner to lose his spool.

An Avalanche Transceiver. This electronic device, like the radiolocation transmitter (RLT) used to locate lost aircraft, instills confidence without being alcoholic. How it works: on sighting an avalanche in your immediate vicinity, you activate your transceiver to beep. Because you are buried under ten feet of snow, your beeper will be audible only to another beeper. This is why you should have remembered to ski with a companion who can beep and be beeped.

Statistics show that a buried person has less than a 50 percent chance of surviving if not found within thirty minutes. You don't have time to wait till someone at the office notices that your chair hasn't been slept in. It will take your companion an average of five minutes to trace your beep to your actual body and wish that you hadn't insisted on carrying the snow shovel ("I paid for it, so I get to carry it, so there!")

What should you do if you are caught beepless and alone in an avalanche that buries you under ten feet of snow? Immobilized upside down. And still wearing your skis. You have several options:

1. Pray for an early spring thaw.
2. Try to think like a polar bear.
3. Eat snow very quickly.

By far the safest place to be on the mountain is with the search and rescue team—off duty. So long as you stay close to another member—marry him if necessary—your chance of getting lost is minimal. Or, if you get lost, you have company that certainly should have known better.

Ski Search and Rescue. What are the qualifications for your joining a ski search and rescue team? First, you should have had some experience with skiing *in bad places.* Where, you ask, do I find bad places if I'm not allowed to go there? Well, we're not going to tell you because the law in this country still forbids assisted suicide. You will just have to stumble upon bad places on your own. And don't say we sent you.

If you have already survived skiing in bad places, the next things you should consider before trying to join a search-and-rescue team are:

1. Am I prepared to be part of a *volunteer* organization? Usually unpaid? Just doing dangerous work for humanitarian reasons difficult to explain to someone who is sane? Like my mother?

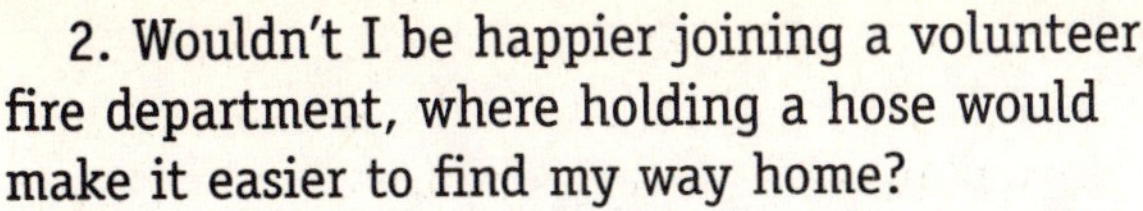

2. Wouldn't I be happier joining a volunteer fire department, where holding a hose would make it easier to find my way home?

3. How do I feel about being *interviewed* in front of news media cameras without pancake makeup? Will I need to have my teeth capped? If so, is this tax deductible? Under Medical or Charitable?

4. Finally, am I just suffering from a *Savior Complex?* Looking for an alternative to the Salvation Army because I don't like the uniform?

If you are satisfied with your answers to these questions, and your doctor has confirmed that you have a sense of direction, by all means make search and rescue your goal as a skier. It is a noble service and will go a long way towards compensating for vices that you have no intention of giving up.

It is clear that mountain skiing offers a wealth of opportunities to die young. Or middle-aged. Old people really should find some other kind of euthanasia. There is already too much garbage being left by back-country skiers without the added bother of having to inform next of kin.

In fact, too many Nordic skiers seem to plunge into the sport as an alternative to making a Living Will. "Just let me go," they appear to be saying, "with no heroic measures, except maybe a hot buttered rum."

Which brings us to the fundamental question: *"Why do you want to ski without first consulting a licensed psychiatrist?"*

Ski Search and Rescue Rule #24: Once the patient is stabilized, get him/her down the mountain as quickly as possible.

CHAPTER 12

To Ski or Not to Ski

What's Your Motivation?

NOW THAT YOU have spent $3,290.96 on ski equipment, $545.20 on ski lessons, $315.80 on season's tickets, $500 on accident insurance and $1.99 on a prayer mat—*why* are you taking up skiing? Have you asked yourself this question? Unless you understand your motivation, how do you expect to relate your injury to Workers Compensation?

Of the following motivations for skiing, choose one (at least):

- ❑ I want a winter exercise more prestigious than shoveling snow off my driveway.
- ❑ My mother knitted me a toque, and I look silly in it bowling.
- ❑ I have a death wish but would like it to come as a surprise.
- ❑ I had two lengths of shiplap left over from building the chicken coop.
- ❑ I am succumbing to peer pressure and hoping to be mistaken for nobility.
- ❑ I think I'd look good in a neck brace.
- ❑ It's better to have an icicle drop into your pants than never to have loved at all.
- ❑ I am a practicing masochist looking for a winter substitute for golf.
- ❑ I hope to meet someone who will love me when I'm blue—literally.

The last of these motivations can be the most compelling.

Reason: skiing offers an incomparable opportunity to be projected into the arms of a gorgeous stranger, legs entangled, without your having to qualify for pro wrestling. We all yearn to meet someone we can look up to. Where better than on a stretcher?

Your skiing may well be a response to a subconscious urge to mate. Do you have, hidden in your room, videos like *Endless Powder?* Watching them while your mother has gone looking for a job? Don't feel guilty. The snow goose, among other waterfowl, flies north to mate. There appears to be something about cold and ice and very long nights that gives reproduction an advantage over common sense.

It is no shame if you have the same migratory instinct, especially if you have a natural tendency to travel in a V-formation.

If you are a female, you may be drawn to skiing because it offers a great chance to meet a high-earning male who is still young enough to become sexually aroused without a prosthesis. For downhill skiing in North America, statistics show gender to split between 60 percent male, 40 percent female. This research involved the removal of many layers of clothing, but is considered reliable within .3 percent.

The imbalance is also attractive to many young men who can't believe that a woman would be so determined to find commitment as to pursue it into the mountains. Men feel safer on a vertical slope than in an urban singles bar. Their *sang-froid* is of course unwarranted. Women travel great distances—from Australia, South Africa, Florida—in order to find men whose instinct for self-preservation has been weakened by a shortage of oxygen.

If you plan to be a *male* skier, your enthusiasm may stem from hoping that your form on the slopes will come across as a courting display, impressing women who have failed to respond to your juggling three grapefruit.

Whether you are male, female or undecided, it may help you to understand your urge to ski if you study statistics provided by the Canadian Ski Council. The Ski Council will appreciate your doing this. It went to a lot of trouble interviewing people who mumbled because their lips were frozen.

First, the average annual income of active alpine skiers in Canada is $56,000. Does this mean you are disqualified from active skiing if you make only $55,500? Certainly not. Someone else is making $56,500, but is he any happier? Who knows? The Ski Council didn't ask. All it has established, really, is that some skiers are goofing off from a well-paid job. There are no statistics to prove it, but evidence suggests that 90 percent of sick leaves taken by office workers coincide with the first skiable fall of snow on the mountains.

It is also no coincidence that the influenza season starts in the same month (December) as the ski season. Or that it ends (in May) with the snow's disappearing. People whose illness strikes during summer months are usually golfers, victims of the eighteen-hole flu.

Perhaps you are one of the 25 percent of skiers who say they are employed only part time. If so, you will not be able to get sick as often as those with a steady job. Part-time jobs are said to be the employment of the future. It is hard to say which came first: the decline of the traditional workweek or the ascendancy of the snowboard.

Even more startling is the finding that 37 percent of skiers describe themselves as unemployed. These are in addition to members of the Royal Family. So, being jobless need not inhibit you from joining the crowd on the slope, secure in knowing that one in three belongs to that privileged class known as:

The Ski Bum. Can you ski on welfare? Is the Pope Catholic? Skiing is the most elevating way to take a vow of poverty. How else would one find the time for this religious passion but by being gainfully unemployed? Be happy that you have found a cult that doesn't do nasty things to cats. Yet you have the fundamentalist zeal that would see you prepared to commit group suicide (skiing Mount Etna) before letting a job interfere with your worshipping the Nordic gods: Thor, Odin, K2 and Labatt.

Next to Islam, Skiing is the fastest-growing religion in North America.

For its adherents, it is forbidden to drink water (a degraded form of snow). Women skiers who wear short skirts will be escorted to the nearest bar and questioned. The Skier who marries a non-Skier may not have children on the lift.

When the Skier prays, it is for an early arrival of the next ice age. And with it, skiing in Hawaii. He crusades against global warming and the resultant retreat of snow and ice to mountains too far north to be reached before lunch.

Ski Bum Jungle

This concern about the greenhouse effect on the spread of the ski gospel conflicts with the felling of old-growth forest to relieve crowding on the ski slopes. If you are a devout environmentalist, how can you also support the clear-cutting needed for new ski facilities? Thinking too much about this evangelical dichotomy can make your face break out. The only way to assuage your conscience is to plant a tree every weekend that you spend skiing. Don't plant it where you will ski into it. You're already in enough trouble.

This devotion to the Immaculate Conception of skiing is facilitated by getting a job at the ski resort. Thousands of young pilgrims from all parts of the world flock to the ski resorts every November, eager to assume the missionary position. They don't mind how cramped and crude is the staff accommodation. The old song "I've Got My Love to Keep Me Warm" could serve as the oratorio of ski-resort workers. Because inhibitions tend to become more relaxed in ski towns like Whistler and Aspen, morals follow the body on the downhill.

As if the rustic Bavarian ambiance were not aphrodisiac enough for the resort worker, 81 percent of skiers own their own homes. Not all the homes are detached houses. The single-family dwelling of some skiers is a pup tent. Ask for photos.

Also to keep in mind: the average age of the North American skier is twenty-eight, and he or she is making nearly $60,000 a year. Chances are good that you will meet someone who is ready to move up to a really nice apartment. If you already own a really nice apartment, watch out for the 19 percent who are renting. Their helping you chase your skis may not be entirely because you look sex-worthy.

Sex and the Single Skier. Is it possible that by skiing you will meet someone who finds you sexually attractive regardless of your status as a homeowner? Yes, of course! One of the glories of the alpine sport is that, on the slope, it is impossible to tell prince from pauper. Or even make a positive identification as to gender. For this reason, unless you are bisexual, you should avoid falling in love with a great brace of buns, only to be heartbroken when the owner enters the wrong washroom.

Here it should be noted that skiing is one sport that does not facilitate male bonding. Or female bonding. It is a prime source of heterosexual bonding. With the addition of a horse-drawn sleigh ride, the bonding can last for weeks, not to say days.

On this score, it is fair to say that if Casanova were alive today, he would be operating on planks. At the ski resort. Which has largely replaced the royal courts of Europe as the fulcrum of seduction, the place where the rich and famous get down and dirty. The great facilitator: *the après ski.*

Après ski is the French term meaning "after doing something before doing what I am really after." For many skiers, the après ski is the most important part of the skiing experience. Some get so aroused that the grave accent (`) becomes acute (´) . . .

I ski, you ski,
we all ski
for whiski. (Old Nordic drinking song)

Après ski as depicted in brochures.

It was either Dorothy Parker or Robert Benchley who said, "Let's get you out of those wet clothes and into a dry martini." Neither Parker nor Benchley was a notable skier, but their attitude towards damp garb, and the pleasure to be gained from getting out of it as quickly as possible in front of a hot toddy, catches the spirit of the après ski.

[Note: Do not impair the impression that you are a ski-resort sophisticate by trying to throw a log on the gas fireplace. Leave your logs at home. And should someone attractive say to you, "Baby, light my fire," don't take it as an invitation to practice your Boy Scout or Girl Guide camping skills.]

Despite the popularity of the après ski, few skiing manuals explain the technique required to become a world-class après skier. Unless you know how to carve your turn into the hotel lounge, having first remembered to remove your skis, you may have wasted the hundreds of dollars you were persuaded to spend on your après-ski designer sweatshirt, your après-ski lingerie and your après-ski Eau de Lite.

Après skiing may occur

1. after dark, or
2. in broad daylight.

The simpler to understand is the *daylight* après ski. This consists of doing one run (or less) and spending the rest of the day on the resort restaurant deck, soaking up the sun and other warming bodies. To bask on the terrace is an excellent way to strengthen the elbow in case you go skiing again. You should, however, wear your beeper. If you happen to fall off the deck into a snowbank, your survival could depend on communicating with your server.

Or—and this is the main attraction of spring skiing—you can find a quiet spot off-slope to have a picnic. You make what is called a snow bed, an arrangement of ski poles and skis pushed into the snow to screen off curious onlookers

Après ski in reality.

who have nothing better to do than herringbone laboriously up the hill. Laugh noiselessly.

There is no reason why your picnic should not include food as well as drink. It is one of the few times when you can enjoy a picnic without competition from ants and/or wasps. And your sunscreen should trap most of the blackflies.

The *nocturnal* après ski is even more popular than the daylight picnic, since the light is poorer. Love ballads like Jo Stafford's "It Happened in Sun Valley" refer to the romantic scenario of the après ski rather than wiping out on the nursery run.

The cordial atmosphere of the ski-resort lounge favors the après-ski move called "coming on" to another après skier. There is no need to be introduced by your mother or your pastor unless they too are up enjoying a dirty weekend. The verbal exchange gives fresh meaning to "the snow line" . . .

"Do you ski here often?" Not too imaginative.

"Do you think of yourself as a consenting adult?" Iffy. You may be risking a slap in the face. Après skiing is a dangerous sport, but few people—women especially—feel that close to death to be ready to jump into bed with the first person who offers to buy them a drink. Too many male après skiers think that foreplay is something required of male golfers ("Fore! Okay, we can play through.") Not so.

"I couldn't help admiring your respiration at this altitude." Better, but not surefire. To be safe, restrict physical references to snow conditions. There are so many types of snow—corn, crust, ice, powder, spring, tracked, wet, windblown and none—that the simple question, "Hey, what kind of snow do you think we'll have tomorrow?" gives ample opportunity for eye contact, comparison of weather forecasts and the hopeful exchange of room numbers.

WARNING: The person who appears glamorous to you during the après ski may look quite plain at sea level and downright ugly under water. When you're under the influence of snowflakes on eyelashes, you may not have found the best time to get engaged. Also, some people who are bewitchingly graceful on skis walk like a duck when off them.

ANOTHER WARNING (stronger): Because the après-ski atmosphere loosens the Velcro straps on inhibitions, you may be tempted to do things that you would consider profligate at your local community center. Such as *going all the way*. How far *is* that? Can you make it without a map? HOW DO YOU GET BACK?

These questions involve moral values, which your authors do not pretend to have. What can be said with some certainty is that mountain air, being low in particulates, heightens the libido. One remedy (anecdotal): spike your hot chocolate with a dash of saltpeter.

Your guide for the après ski: if you feel yourself succumbing to carnal temptation, phone Mom or take a cold shower, whichever you can do for a quarter.

CHAPTER 13

Whither the Faith!

Is Skiing Going Downhill?

THIS MUCH WE KNOW: the major religions of the world are Catholicism, Protestantism, Judaism, Hinduism, Muhammadanism, Buddhism and Skiism. Of these, Skiism is the most likely to have adherents whose zeal borders on the fanatic. Skiers gladly give up all their worldly goods in order to join in the religious ecstasy of a few days on the hills. Mother Teresa, some believe, started out as a Skier, but converted to Roman Catholicism when she lost faith in her wax.

But the faith is in peril.

Skiing's Vatican—the National Ski Areas Association based in Denver, Colorado—has issued a warning: "A growing percentage of tourists who go to ski resorts don't necessarily ski, or don't ski regularly." This is like visiting the Sistine Chapel without looking at the ceiling.

Without the saintly dedication to strapping on the boards and purging the mind of earthly pleasure, skiing becomes mere pastime. The ski resort is losing its identity as a Lourdes where the faithful arrive hale and leave on crutches.

In order to attract these mere pleasure-seekers, resorts are having to install expensive amenities like heated lifts. The tourist balks at having to sit on a cold seat, failing to understand that mortifying the flesh is an essential part of skiing's Puritanism. These sybarites also demand first-class restaurants with printed menus and a chef who spends at least part of his day in the kitchen.

These furbelows cost money. Staff must be paid when they are not allowed to wait on table wearing their skis. Changing sheets on beds entails chambermaids who may have heard that employment normally involves wages.

Hence, the ski resorts must become more and more pricey. Some already cater almost exclusively to movie stars, royalty and union plumbers. The affluent class. Worse, they must become all-season resorts with tennis courts, golf courses, health spas and satellite villages whose town fathers regard snow as something of a nuisance to be cleared away as quickly as possible to admit another tourist bus. The ordinary skier who wanders into such a complex may feel intimidated, afraid to belly up to a bar lest he be denied service for not having garlic on his breath.

Virtually extinct is the Mom-and-Pop ski facility, which basically consisted of a sign indicating which way was up, and a second sign: YIELD TO BEARS. This is where low-income folk could learn to ski on cheap or borrowed boards without fear that they were degrading the path of the Crown Prince of Japan. There were no security persons patrolling, quick to eject anyone not displaying conspicuous consumption.

The devout skier may also see heresy in the cult of snowboarding, to be regarded with the same hostility as the Church of Rome felt in dealing with Henry the Eighth. But in neither case has excommunication restored authority. Yearn as ye may for an update on the Inquisition, the ski rack will remain innocuous.

Too, you must find it in your heart to forgive your ski resort when it cuts down several hundred hectares of old-growth forest in order to create the new Widow-maker downhill. Don't think of it as a double tragedy when you ski into a tree stump. There is no way that anyone can trace that butt to you.

Remember, there are still plenty of big trees left. Maybe not on *your* mountain. But certainly on several mountains in rural Patagonia, where people can't afford to join the elect.

The Mission. Instead of becoming guilt-ridden—whether because of the cost to nature or your bank account—you, the postulant skier, should focus on the power and the glory of Skiing. Yes, the faith does merit being capitalized. As an international institution, drawing together people from all parts of the world, Skiing may well replace the United Nations Organization. The UN was a good try, but the ski resort does it better.

Is this not, then, the spiritual force behind the hegira to the mountaintop? To be nearer, O God, to thee, and ski? Is this not why it is not uncommon to see a skier drop to his knees, taking the Lord's name in vain while his skis take off to perdition?

What could be more chaste than fresh powder snow? Only with this pure love can you have spiritual

intercourse, confident that you are the first, and that this is one relationship that won't land you on *Oprah*.

Not the least of the sublime experience is that skiing gives a grown adult the rejuvenation of catching snowflakes on the tongue and on the expense account. These are the glorious moments to be recalled when we are too old to telemark and are sitting by the fire, telling our grandchildren lies about our schussing by the light of a full moon, down the longest run in the Rockies. And we shall inspire them with skiing's effulgent message:

Where there's life there's slope.